CETAMURA DEL CHIANTI

Cities and Communities of the Etruscans

NANCY THOMSON DE GRUMMOND AND
LISA C. PIERACCINI, SERIES EDITORS

This series was initiated to open discussion and ask questions about what defines an Etruscan city. How did Etruscan cities arise, and what can they tell us about urbanism in ancient Italy? How did Etruscan cities create their own identities, and how are they similar to or different from each other? These queries can be applied to the study of the "Twelve Peoples of the Etruscans," a conventional historical term used in ancient Rome to refer to the most important cities of the Etruscans, the majority of which can be identified today. The aim of this book series is to stimulate and contribute to current vigorous debates concerning Etruscan culture and art, state formation, urban development, and the socioeconomic characteristics of settlements in Etruria.

To understand the major Etruscan cities better, it is also vital to look at the numerous smaller settlements and discuss their similarities to and differences from one another and the larger cities nearby. How can we trace how Etruscan communities developed differently from cities? Did these settlements play a distinctive role in networks of trade in comparison to the large cities? Did smaller communities produce the same arts as their sizable neighbors? Did they worship different Etruscan gods from those of the great cities?

By asking such questions we hope to access the social, religious, economic, architectural, artistic, and civic fabric of each Etruscan city and community. This approach highlights the unique Etruscan contributions to ancient Italy without relying heavily on the traditional methodologies that look to Greece or Rome to explain Etruscan customs, culture, art, and traditions.

CETAMURA DEL CHIANTI

NANCY THOMSON
DE GRUMMOND

University of Texas Press
AUSTIN

This book has been supported by an endowment dedicated to classics and the ancient world and funded by the Areté Foundation; the Gladys Krieble Delmas Foundation; the Dougherty Foundation; the James R. Dougherty, Jr. Foundation; the Rachael and Ben Vaughan Foundation; and the National Endowment for the Humanities.

Printed in the United States of America
First edition, 2020

♾ The paper used in this book meets the minimum requirements of ANSI/NISO Z39.48-1992 (R1997) (Permanence of Paper).

Library of Congress Cataloging-in-Publication Data

Names: De Grummond, Nancy Thomson, author.
Title: Cetamura del Chianti / Nancy Thomson de Grummond.
Description: First edition. | Austin : University of Texas Press, 2020. |
Series: Cities and communities of the Etruscans |
Includes bibliographical references and index.
Identifiers: LCCN 2019007788
ISBN 978-1-4773-1910-9 (cloth : alk. paper)
ISBN 978-1-4773-1993-2 (paper : alk. paper)
ISBN 978-1-4773-1911-6 (library e-book)
ISBN 978-1-4773-1912-3 (nonlibrary e-book)
Subjects: LCSH: Cetamura del Chianti Site (Italy) | Excavations (Archaeology)—Italy—Cetamura del Chianti Site. | Etruscans—Italy—Cetamura del Chianti Site. | Romans—Italy—Cetamura del Chianti Site. | Italy—Antiquities.
Classification: LCC DG70.C398 D4 2020 | DDC 937/.568—dc23
LC record available at https://lccn.loc.gov/2019007788

doi:10.7560/319109

CONTENTS

ILLUSTRATIONS

Maps

Figures

FOREWORD

With this volume we introduce a new feature in the Cities of the Etruscans series of the University of Texas Press, whereby we will expand the examination of Etruscan habitation sites by incorporating studies of single, smaller Etruscan communities. Our series began with the idea of creating volumes dedicated to the urban centers of the Etruscans, considering that ancient texts tell us that the Etruscans had an alliance of Twelve Peoples or city-states. Such sites, identifiable through a combination of literary and archaeological evidence, raise questions about the formation and development of urban environments and the accommodation of large populations within cities that played a highly significant role in historical events. Abundant material evidence both helps to establish the identity of these towns and their inhabitants and allows researchers to address a wide range of topics related to society, religion, economy, trade, art, and government.

Thus far in the series the volumes on Caere and Veii have been completed, and as we worked on these volumes we realized the value of including Etruscan settlements not necessarily defined as a city proper. In this way the series as a whole can offer a full and varied examination of Etruscan life, culture, and habitation. In the region inhabited by the Etruscans there are numerous smaller specialized habitation sites, varying in size and population, that served such varied functions as fortress, sanctuary, trade center, harbor, and production zone (or sometimes combining two or three such functions). These settlements may be situated close to urban areas or found in the remote countryside. Regardless of their location, they greatly enhance our understanding of Etruscan settled life. They fill in an important gap, providing significant data about communities outside of city walls. It is our hope that by incorporating this expanded view of Etruscan cities and communities, our series will also provide a model for how scholars can better approach the ancient Mediterranean as a whole.

Cetamura del Chianti is thus the subject of the first volume in the newly named series, Cities and Communities of the Etruscans. This hilltop settlement may serve to illustrate the type of information that comes from examining the smaller communities and how such data can broaden our view about the larger settlements. Cetamura is located almost exactly at the crossroads of four major Etruscan cities that are to be studied in the series: Chiusi, Arezzo, Volterra, and Fiesole. Without Cetamura there is quite a large gap in habitation between these cities. Further, since Cetamura, unlike those four sites, is not inhabited in modern times, it offers the chance to follow up on discoveries without the frustration that comes when a modern town and its installations block progress in excavation. It also offers the chance to excavate a larger percentage of the known site than will ever be possible for some of the great cities because they lie under modern ones.

In regard to time period, Cetamura is exceptional for what it reveals about the era when some large cities were disintegrating in southern Etruria amid wars with the Romans during the fourth to first centuries BCE. Very likely some of its inhabitants came from the south to the north with the understanding that there would be a new mode of living on the hilltops, one that would allow them still to prosper in difficult times. They created an artisans' zone where a number of crafts were practiced side by side, a pattern that may have been more common than has been recognized in the archaeological record of the cities.

Cetamura also provides a model for habitation in which a sanctuary was created immediately adjoining the artisans' zone, and we have clear evidence that the artisans frequented the sanctuary. This situation allows us to focus on the religious practice of a specialized stratum of society. The Cetamura sanctuary is unique for many reasons, not least of which is the fact that it fostered cult worship of Lur and Leinth, two relatively little known Etruscan deities. Are they the main deities typical for a small community like Cetamura, as opposed to major city protectors such as Uni, Tinia, or Menerva?

The two wells of Cetamura are exceptional for providing stratigraphic columns in which it is possible to follow not only the cultural development but also the nature of the environment of Chianti over a period of some six hundred years. A staggering amount of wood, some of it worked, and as an assemblage quite rare, was retrieved from the two wells. Studies of pollen and seeds also vividly reveal the history of the oak forests and the vineyards of Chianti from Etruscan to Roman times. In fact the site is of the greatest interest for what it tells us about the oft-discussed issues around the "Romanization" of the Etruscans. One of the latest-known Etruscan settlements, Cetamura provides crystal-clear evidence of the moment when it became the property of a Roman, evidently one of the soldiers of Octavian who retired right after the Battle of Actium in 31 BCE.

There are numerous other Etruscan settlements, some smaller and some larger, that deserve to be studied with a close-up lens in the way that Cetamura is examined in this volume, so that their special contributions to this civilization may be recognized and integrated into the study of habitation within a larger archaeological scope. The aim is to provide a spectrum of sites, not so much to contrast city and countryside (though this is of course important) as to try to understand the relationship between sites of different sizes, functions, economic and social systems, and environments and how they may have been drawn together in networks of exchange of goods and ideas. The picture we have of Etruscan civilization at present is very rich but is also notoriously still riddled with gaps that limit our understanding. Incorporating the smaller communities, often fascinating in themselves, into the larger study of Etruscan habitation can provide fuller and more detailed comprehension of life in ancient Etruria.

Nancy Thomson de Grummond
Lisa C. Pieraccini

PREFACE AND ACKNOWLEDGMENTS

The present volume is intended to give a concise general introduction in English to the Etruscan remains at the ancient community of Cetamura del Chianti (Siena) in Italy. The main focus, within the University of Texas Press series on the Cities and Communities of the Etruscans, is to demonstrate that a settlement such as Cetamura can provide novel perspectives on society, economy, religion, industry, and other cultural aspects in an Etruscan rural context that appears to be very different from what we see at major Etruscan urban sites like Caere and Veii.

A much-abbreviated version of this text was first published in Italian as *Cetamura del Chianti: Una communità etrusca* (Florence: Edifir, 2017), in connection with an exhibition at the Museo Archeologico Nazionale di Firenze (MAF), "I pozzi delle meraviglie: Nuove scoperte a Cetamura del Chianti," on display from June 9 to September 30, 2017. That Italian text was conceived as a complement to the exhibition catalog in English, *Wells of Wonders: New Discoveries at Cetamura del Chianti* (Florence: Edifir, 2017).

I am grateful to Edifir for allowing the University of Texas Press to incorporate content from the version originally published in Italian. Scholarly research is here presented with great attention to details and documentation in endnotes, resulting in a different kind of research contextualization that matches closely what has been presented as ideal in the University of Texas Press volumes on the Etruscan cities of Caere and Veii.

It is truly impossible to thank properly the many individuals who contributed to the presentation of material in this volume. The principal researchers are recognized in chapter 8, "Cetamura after Antiquity," and I know I speak for all members of the team in expressing gratitude to the Italian entities and administrators that have unfailingly supported our efforts: the Ministero dei Beni e delle Attività Culturali of the state of Italy and its wing for archaeology, the Soprintendenza Archeologia Belle Arti e Paesaggio (SABAP) per le province di Siena, Grosseto e Arezzo (Arch. Anna Di Bene, Soprintendente), along with Florida State University (Tallahassee, Florida), especially the entity of International Programs (Jim Pitts, Director) and Studio Arts College International in Florence (SACI; Steven Brittan, President). We acknowledge the encouragement and enthusiasm of the Badia a Coltibuono and the Comune of Gaiole in Chianti (SI), within the territory of which Cetamura is located, and important financial support from the Consorzio Vino Chianti Classico, which has helped with urgently important research on the ancient grape seeds found in the wells of Cetamura. It is a pleasure to thank here the many individual donors who have supported the research and contributed toward the successful exhibition.

Several individual names cannot be omitted from the acknowledgments. Most recently, Frank Nero, Director of the Florida State University Study Abroad Program in Florence, with the encouragement of the US Consul General to Florence, Benjamin V. Wohlauer, has renewed the commitment of the study center to the Cetamura project, which began originally in 1973 as a course in the FSU Florence program and in 1978 became an independent summer field school. The resources of the superb staff, facilities, and student body of the study center have been of the greatest value for a new agenda involving the creation of a museum for Cetamura. Michele Pescini, the mayor of Gaiole in Chianti, has been an ardent supporter of the excavations and with the town council of Gaiole has recently designated space for a museum for Cetamura and the origins of Chianti in the handsome restored building of the former Cantine Ricasoli in the center of Gaiole, now named the Museo Civico Alle Origini del Chianti.

Mario Iozzo, Director of the Museo Archeologico Nazionale di Firenze, validated the importance of the material remains of Cetamura by welcoming the exhibition of "I pozzi delle meraviglie" to the museum. Pierluigi Giroldini, formerly *funzionario* from SABAP for Cetamura, constantly assisted with every kind of problem faced; Jacopo Tabolli now serves as *funzionario* in the same role with no less enthusiasm and effectiveness. He has been a dedicated ally in following the procedures associated with the creation of the museum. Nòra Marosi of SACI performed an enormous service to Cetamura and to ancient archaeology by her diligent labors in conserving and restoring a wide range of objects from the site, and by locating and contacting experts who could assist in numerous ways with the special needs of the Cetamura research. She "discovered" the firm of Ichnos: Archeologia, Ambiente e Sperimentazione at Montelupo Fiorentino (Francesco Cini, President), which carried out the arduous excavations in two wells at Cetamura, and established contact with our principal artist, Rosalba Settesoldi, who has created hundreds of drawings of artifacts from Cetamura, some of which are featured in this volume. Many of the photographs of artifacts included here were made by Professor Ken Kobre, a graduate of Florida State University who attended the FSU Study Center at Florence in 1966 at the time of the great flood and who offered his services gratis for the catalogue and this book. Peter Krafft, formerly of FSU, has created all of the final site maps since 1983. Kaitlin Rizzo, a recent graduate of FSU and program assistant for both the Florence and Cetamura programs, took care of final tasks in photography.

Giovanna Bagnasco Gianni, Director of excavations at the major Etruscan city site of Tarquinia, has never failed to show interest in the community site of Cetamura and to contribute when asked to the interpretation of the research. Without her collaboration, my own understanding of the site would be greatly limited.

Nancy Thomson de Grummond

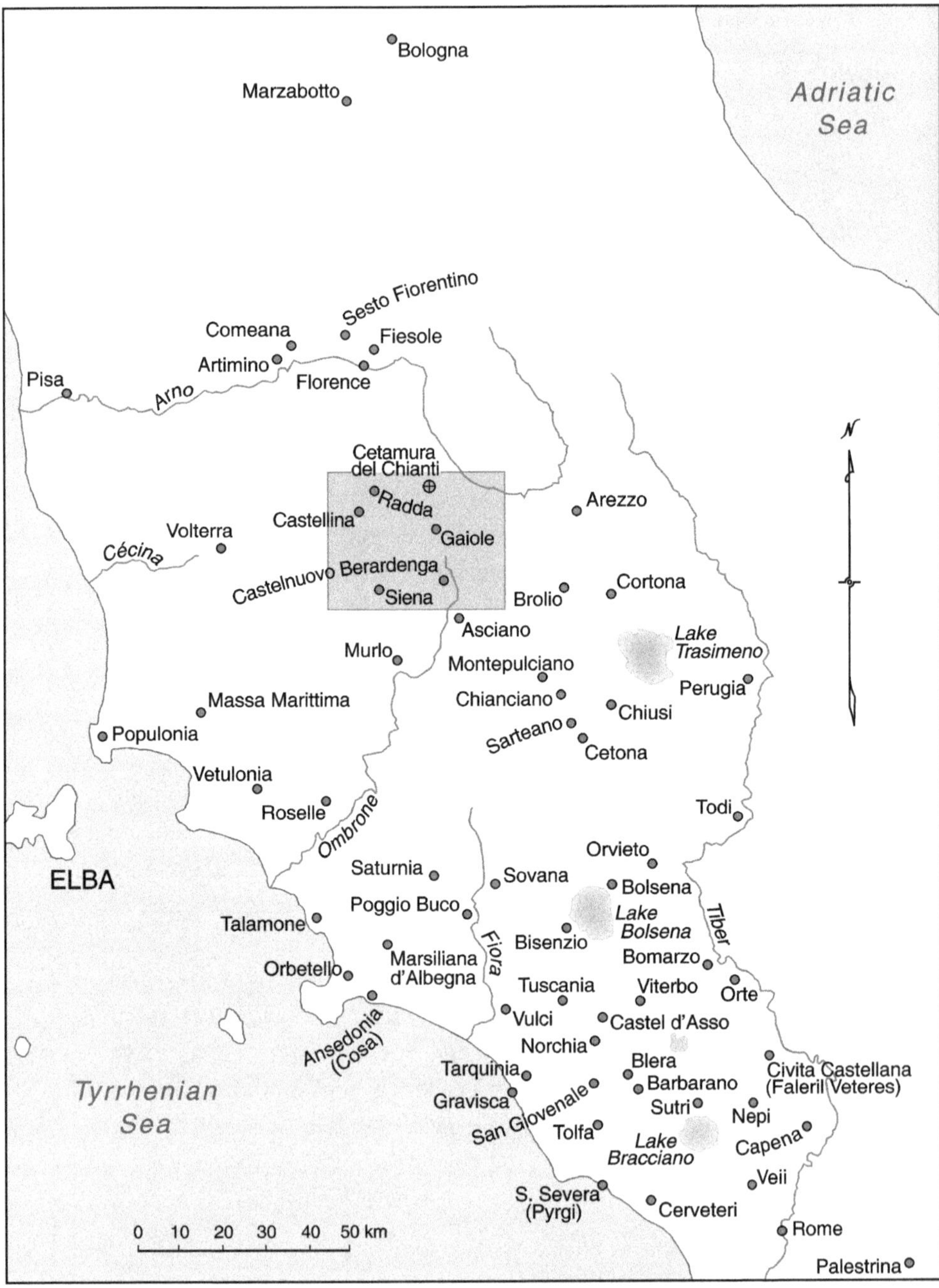

1. Map of Etruscan sites, showing locations of Chianti and Cetamura.

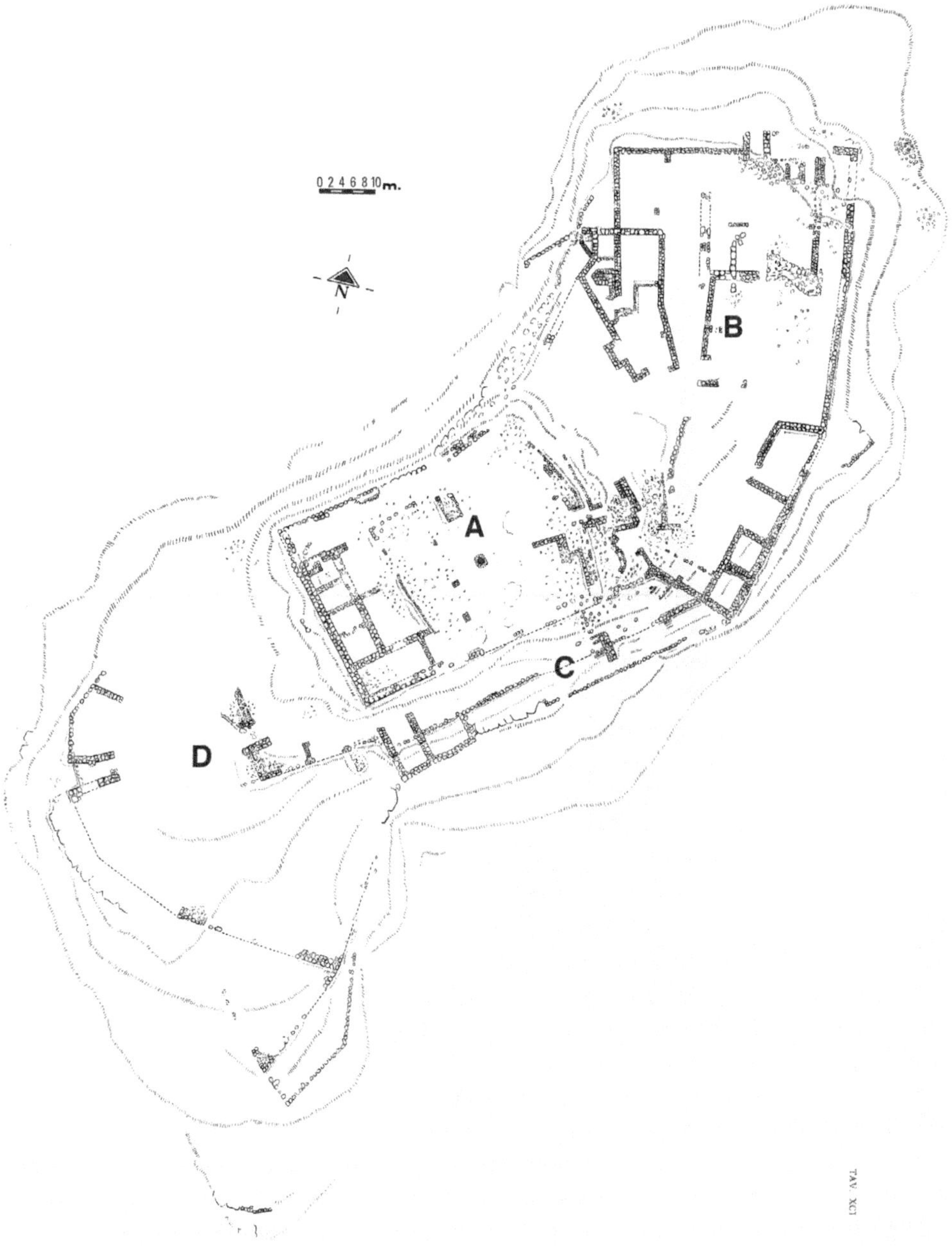

2. Map of the site of Cetamura, by Alvaro Tracchi (1978).

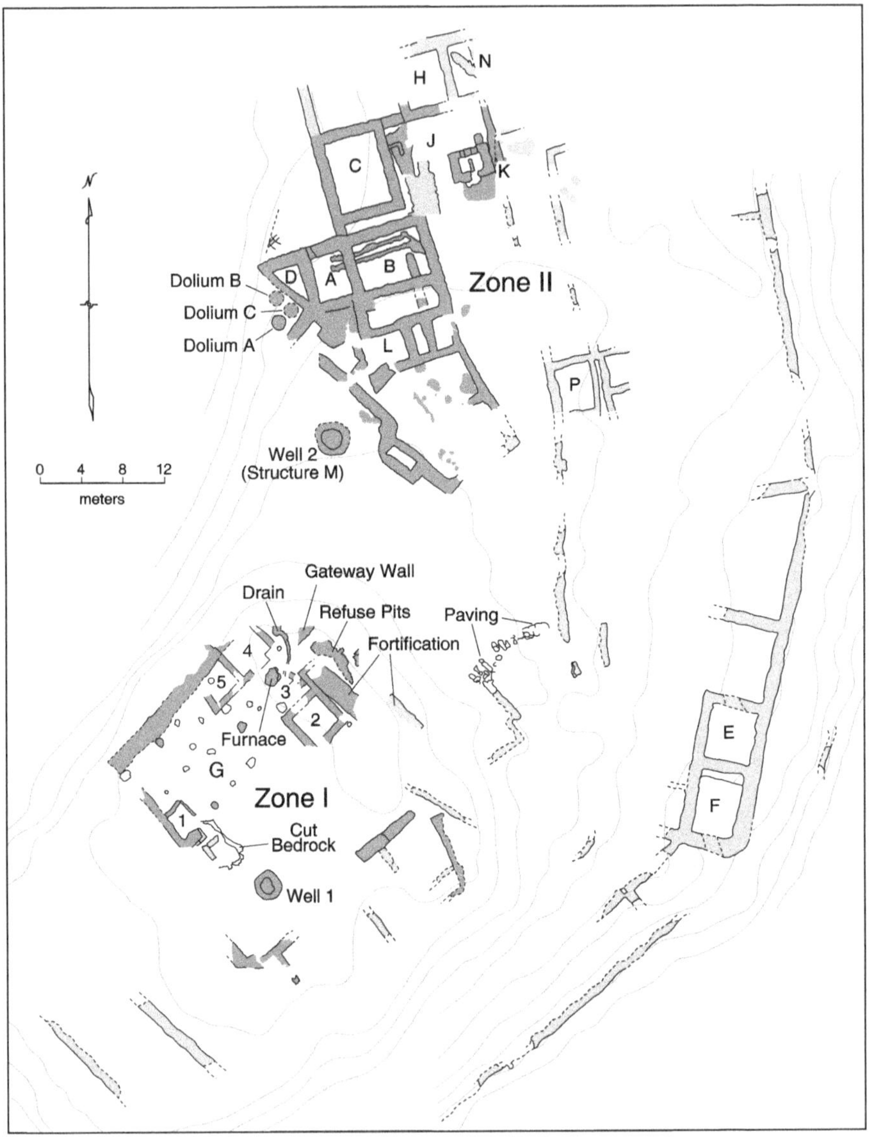

3. General site map of Cetamura (2018).

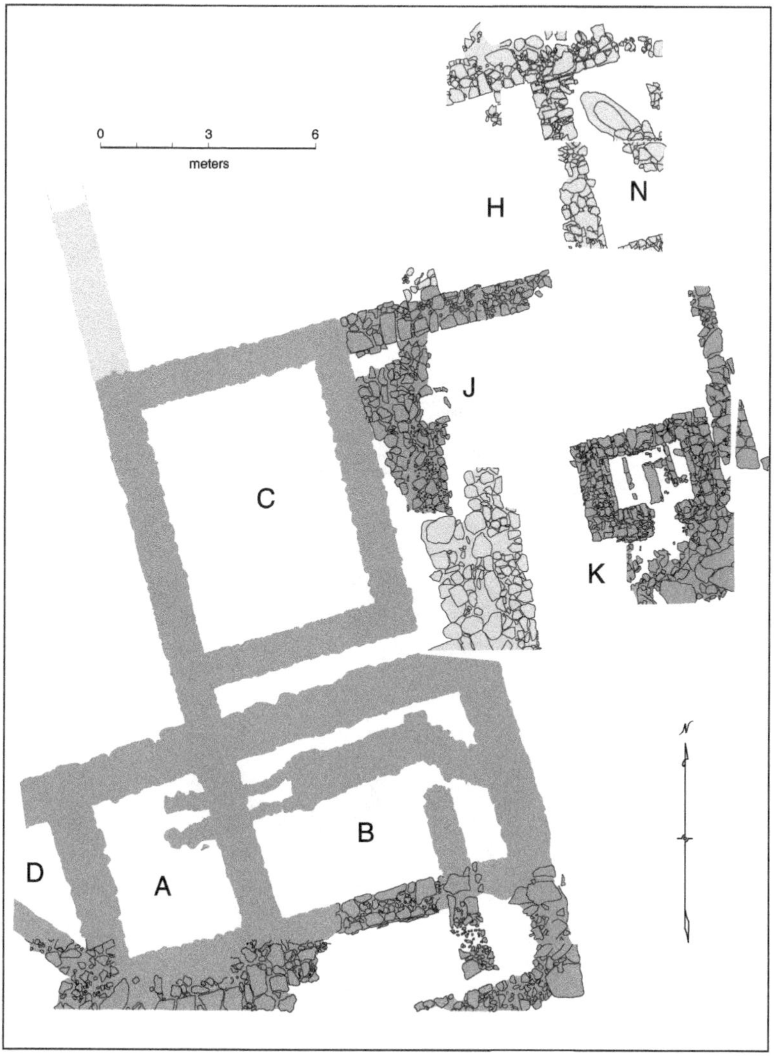

4. Map of Zone II, Artisans' Quarter.

5. Map of Zone II, Sanctuary (Structure L) and Structures A, B, D, and M.

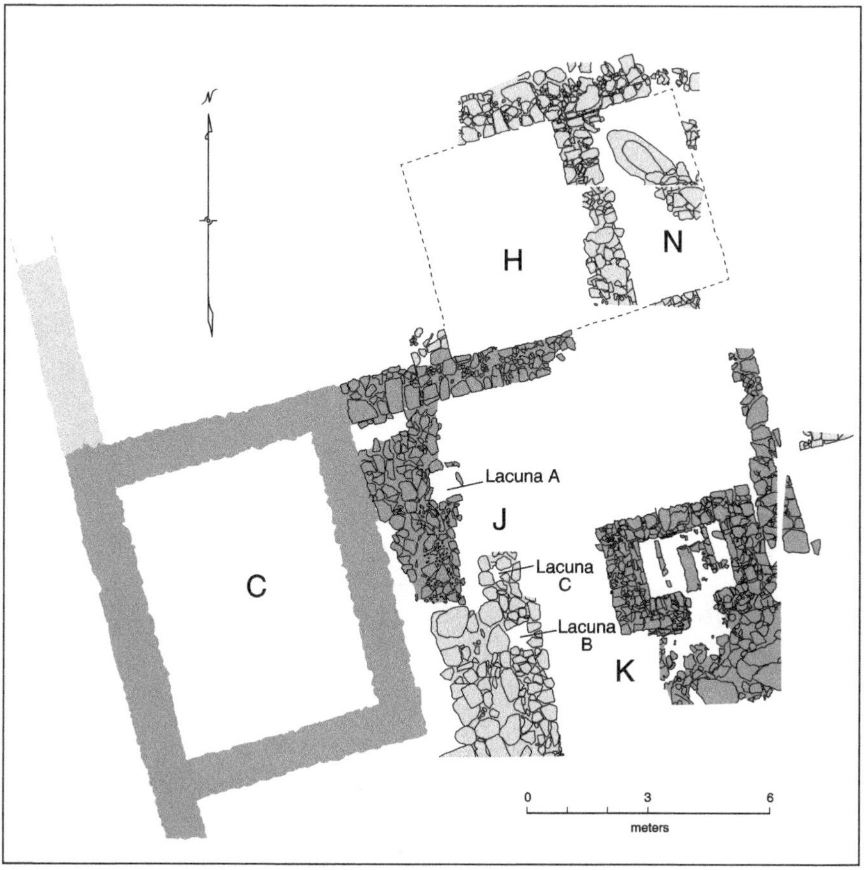

6. Map of Structures C, J, K, H, and N.

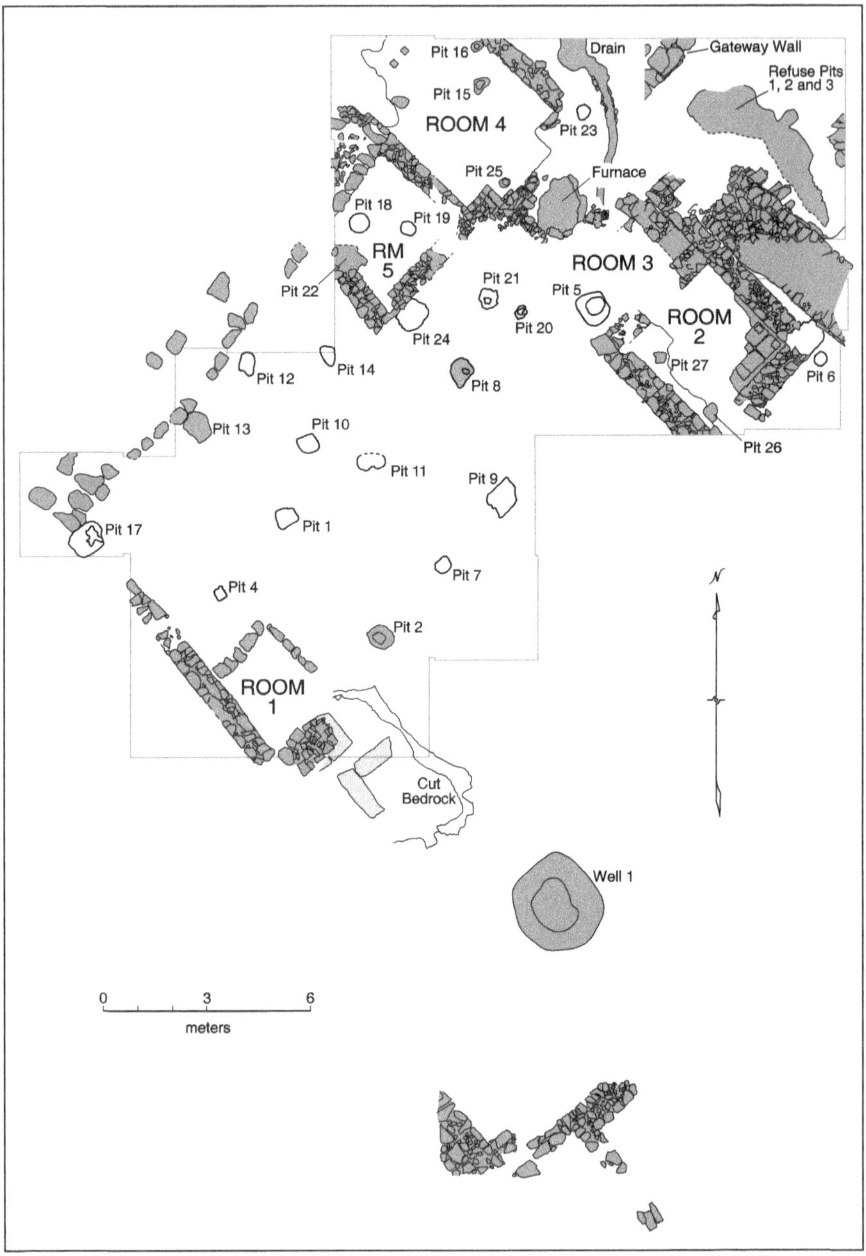

7. Map of Zone I, Area G.

CETAMURA
DEL
CHIANTI

1
Introduction

Cetamura is a hill located in Tuscany, in the heart of the original zone of production of Chianti Classico wine, ca. 20 kilometers northeast of Siena, on the property of the Badia a Coltibuono in the Comune of Gaiole in Chianti Storico. Its highest point has been recorded at 695 meters above sea level, placing it among the higher ridges in the chain of the Chianti Mountains. In many ways the spot is at a junction of elements (see map 1), connecting with other ridges that create a watershed with rivers to the north (the Arno and its tributaries) and to the south (the Ombrone and its tributaries). Intersecting roads would have led to major Etruscan sites at Volterra and Populonia (east), Arretium (Arezzo; west), Faesulae (Fiesole; north), and Clusium (Chiusi; south). The site is located at latitude 43° (43.4931009) N and longitude 11° (11.43178231) E.[1]

The site was perhaps occupied as late as the fifteenth or sixteenth century, but the ancient remains were quite forgotten until their rediscovery in 1964 by the researcher Alvaro Tracchi, a citizen of nearby San Giovanni Valdarno, who surveyed sites and routes of the Chianti and the Arno Valley to understand the way ancient peoples would have traveled through and around the region.[2] A permit to excavate was granted to Florida State University, and the site was opened on September 10, 1973, under the direction of J. J. Reich, and operated by faculty and students from the FSU Study Abroad Program in Florence until 1978, when it was converted into a summer archaeological field school. Nancy de Grummond became the director of the site in 1983 and has remained so until the present.[3] The history of excavation and research is treated in fuller detail in chapter 8, "Cetamura after Antiquity."

The ancient name of the site is unknown. During the Middle Ages, documents of Coltibuono as early as 1066 refer to the site as "Civitamura," i.e., "Wall City."[4] A later text uses the Latin term *castrum*, "castle," to characterize the place, again alluding to substantial walls.[5] There are indeed remains of medieval fortifications on the site, and of the perimeter walls around the two upper levels of the hill at least some go back to antiquity, as may be seen on the map made by Tracchi and in the latest Cetamura maps (see maps 2–3). In any case, it is obvious that the Latin name used in the Middle Ages, Civitamura, gave rise to the modern Italian name of Cetamura (also found as Cetramura).[6]

The investigations of Tracchi and Florida State University have confirmed that the hilltop of Cetamura was a significant point in the Chianti region where there was a conjunction of roadways and water sources. Etruscans settled there to create a center for production of various goods and obviously regarded the site as sacred to the gods.[7] Much of the evidence belongs to a late phase of Etruscan culture, ca. 300 BCE to the first century BCE. The population was probably never very large, not more than five hundred people at any one time. A sanctuary with altars and votive pits has been discovered adjoining an artisans' quarter, and two wells have been excavated, yielding abundant information about lifeways, rituals, and offerings.[8] Research on organic materials preserved in the waters of the two wells reveals much about the flora and fauna of Cetamura; of particular significance are thousands of grape seeds that testify to the importance of the vineyards and point to continuous production of wine from at least as early as ca. 300 BCE down into the period of the later Roman Empire.[9] Extensive evidence for the environment and agriculture in the region helps in developing a detailed picture of the plants and animals associated with this rural Etruscan community.[10]

In the chapters that follow, information will be given in detail on the various aspects of Cetamura noted above. By way of introduction, included here is a brief walk-through of the site to indicate the relationships of the various features and time periods (see maps 3–7) and the principal themes to look for. The hill features two major zones of habitation that have been explored—Zone I, at the top of the hill (ca. 50 × 35 m), and Zone II (ca. 70 × 60 m), situated ca. 3 meters lower down on the north side. Tracchi also recognized two additional, smaller zones on the slopes of the hill (see map 2; labeled C and D), but no scientific excavation has yet been undertaken there.

A timeline of historical background for the study of Cetamura is included in the appendix. The chronology of habitation at Cetamura is well understood, and the following paragraphs detail the periods and features recognized.

There was habitation on the site in the seventh and sixth centuries BCE, during the Etruscan Archaic period. The principal evidence is found in the ceramics, with a moderate amount of bucchero pottery (see fig. 2.1). No structures have been identified; a single post pit on Zone I has been dated to the period (see map 7: Pit 8). Thus there is little to say about the nature of the Archaic habitation.

Next is a period in which the site seems to have been abandoned, in the fifth century BCE. No artifacts or any relevant contexts found at Cetamura belong to this period.

In the second half of the fourth century there is a new Etruscan horizon, datable by means of drinking cups painted with a metallic black gloss (see fig. 2.4) and a number of other contemporary wares. The period is quite conspicuous on the ridge in between Zone I and Zone II, where a deep crevice in the sandstone bedrock was filled with refuse of broken pottery, ash, and animal bone (see maps 3, 7; figs. 2.2–2.10). The nature of the deposit suggests ritual activities, perhaps associated with the cleaning of a sacred area and the subsequent burial of the debris. Remnants of walls suggest that a gate to Zone I was built here at that time (see map 7). The pottery types appear also in the filling of a wide and deep pit in the middle of Zone I (perhaps a quarry) and in the foundation fill of two walls framing a storage area on Zone II (see fig. 4.5). Within that storage area were found the remains of two large storage jars and the imprint of a third (dolia A, B, and C; see map 5; figs. 3.28–3.29).

Near the end of the fourth century BCE or the beginning of the third century BCE a new wave of settlers seems to have arrived and then constructed Well #1 on Zone I and Well #2 on Zone II (see maps 3, 5; figs. 3.1–3.2). Well #1 is a very deep shaft cut into the bedrock to the depth of 32.42 meters below ground level. The shaft is quite irregular—sometimes rectangular, sometimes cylindrical. It acquired, and still takes in, water through seepage in the porous sandstone bedrock. Well #2 is completely different in character. Rather than being roughly cut in the bedrock, it features a finished interior of quasi-isodomic stone walls in a regular cylindrical shaft, going to a depth of 8.32 meters. Both wells are dated from artifactual content and carbon 14 samples. Both have yielded an enormous amount of cultural and ecological evidence that relates directly to Etruscan religious practices at the site and the concurrent activities of the Etruscan artisans, themes that will recur in this volume and that help to draw parallels with other Etruscan cities and communities.

The most abundant remains of Cetamura come from the Late Etruscan period, divided into two phases: Late Etruscan period, Phase I (300–150 BCE), during which were built Structures B, C, and K, all especially associated with an artisans' quarter (see maps 3–4; figs. 3.3–3.5 and 3.13–3.14); and Late Etruscan period, Phase II (150–75 BCE), when Structures A and B (reworked) and Building L were erected (see map 5; figs. 3.13–3.14 and 4.1–4.4). All of the evidence for this Etruscan period, apart from the contents of Well #1, comes from Zone II of the site. Building L is recognizable as a sanctuary dedicated to the Etruscan gods Lur and Leinth, known in inscriptions from Cetamura (see figs. 3.30–3.31). A great quantity of ceramics secure the dating, especially black-gloss vessels from Volterra and red-gloss bowls often referred to as "Volterran presigillata" (see figs. 3.18, 3.20, 3.22–3.23, 3.32, 4.8–4.10). The Artisans' Quarter, which features a ceramics workshop with at least two kilns, Structures J (see maps 3–4; fig. 3.16) and K, seems to have operated throughout the Late (Hellenistic) period. Numerous objects used for spinning and weaving have been found in the area, perhaps indications of a workshop in Structure C, which features a well-designed flagstone pavement (see fig. 3.14). There is also frequent evidence of ritual behavior in this area adjacent to the sanctuary. Structure N yielded evidence of an iron forge (see maps 3–4; fig. 3.21), while Structures A, B, and D were related to water management, with a drain running through the bottom of the three and an overspill drain on the top of the north side of Structure A (see fig. 4.4).

A series of foundation walls made of stones of varying sizes characterize Structure P (see maps 3 and 5). Their date is as yet unknown. On the eastern edge of Zone II are two structures excavated in the 1980s, Structures E and F, which are hypothesized on the basis of ceramic stratigraphy to be Etruscan, of the Late period, but their purpose is unknown. The pottery is mostly modest local ceramics, and some strata contained a good bit of bone. Since nowhere else have actual residences been identified for the Etruscans at Cetamura, Structures E and F present a credible hypothesis for testing as houses.

A growing Roman presence is discernable in the first half of the first century BCE. The final takeover of the land seems to have occurred immediately after Actium, when a veteran of the army of Augustus arrived and buried a jar of silver coins in a pit on Zone I (see figs. 6.3–6.5). Soon after, in the time of Augustus, baths were built, which certainly went through more than one phase (ca. 27 BCE–second century CE). Only a few walls of the baths and segments of a hypocaust system were found *in situ* (see maps 3 and 7; fig. 6.2). On Zone II, ironworking continued in the area of Structure N. Thus we see the continuity of the theme of production on the site of Cetamura into the Roman period.

Well #2 seems to have been cleaned out and reused in the third through fourth centuries CE, during the Late Roman and early medieval period. Numerous broken pitchers belong to these deposits (see figs. 6.13, 7.1). A major episode in the medieval period dates to the late eleventh–early twelfth centuries CE. Heavy foundations (see fig. 8.1), ceramic bread pans, and combed ware as well as carbon 14 dating of wood and documents from Badia a Coltibuono show that there was once a substantial *castrum* (castle) on Zone I, belonging to the Firidolfi Ricasoli family and seemingly demolished around the end of the twelfth century.

The medieval inhabitants seem to have completely reworked Zone I, so that numerous castle walls took the place of any Etruscan structures that may have been there, and of much of the Roman baths and other possible Roman installations. Area G on Zone I seems to be a courtyard of the *castrum*, with side rooms 1 and 5 added at the time (see maps 3 and 7). A rather thick defensive wall of the medieval period stands on the northwest side of Zone I (behind the Roman baths; see fig. 6.2). Numerous huge sandstone blocks randomly scattered along the ridge may belong to a demolished tower. There is no evidence of any further building at Cetamura. There are no modern installations.

The modern path up the hill, on the north side, is probably the same as the one used in ancient times. One would arrive first on Zone II, near Structures K and N, and pass through the area of the sanctuary and the artisans' zone, near which were the storage area with dolia and Well #2. One would proceed south to go up the hill to the high zone, which already in Etruscan times likely would have been a stronghold area. There today are found the scant remains of the earliest habitation of the site amid the remnants of the Roman baths and the rather extensive medieval building.

◎ 2 ◎

Early and Middle Etruscan Periods (Seventh–Fourth Centuries BCE)

A wave of Etruscan travelers climbed the hill of Cetamura sometime in the fourth century BCE and liked what they found enough to decide to settle down there. The mount features a high zone, a small, flat plateau that has a sheer drop on one side and is easy to fortify on the other sides, and at least one lower zone, likewise flat but spreading out and offering more room for various needs of the community (see map 3). A freshwater spring emerged at the base of the hillside, about 200 meters down from the main zone. Beds of clay that could be used in making ceramics lay not far from the base of the hill. As known from studies of the ancient pollen and wood, there was abundant timber on the mount and in the surrounding area, featuring deciduous oaks and other hardwoods such as hornbeam, hazel, beech, and elm, and fruiting trees such as walnut and Cornelian cherry. Wild grasses were abundant, and flowers included crocus, asphodel, and aster. Animal bones from the site show that boar and deer (both red deer and roe deer) were there for the hunting, and among the birds were owl, pigeon, woodcock, swallow, swift, sparrow, and thrush.

Bucchero Pottery

The fourth-century arrivals were not the first Etruscans to be drawn to Cetamura. Characteristic early Etruscan bucchero pottery has been found on the site, especially on the edges of the top plateau, Zone I, and dates to the sixth century BCE and perhaps as early as

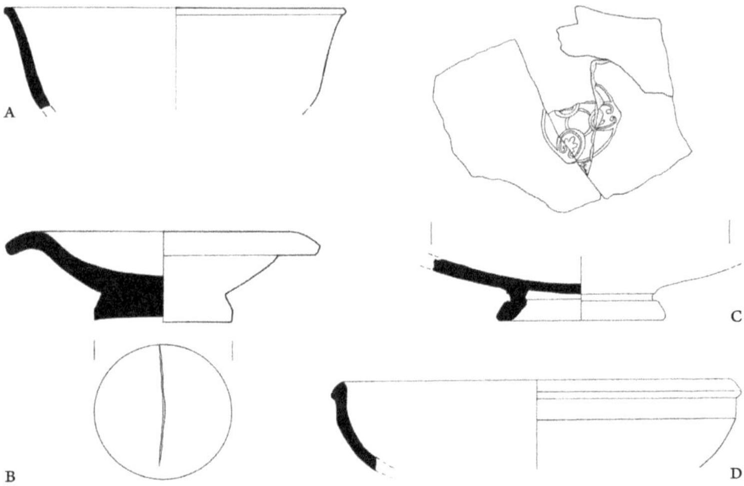

2.1. Bucchero vessels: (A) *kantharos*; (B) saucer; (C) ring-foot plate with stamp; (D) bowl.

the seventh (fig. 2.1).[1] The fabric of this Etruscan ware, made on the wheel, is typically described as finely sifted, burnished on the surface rather than painted, and fired black all the way through. The numerous broken sherds from Cetamura, however, indicate that the interior of the paste may be grainy, varying from black to gray or brown, and the surface may be matte rather than shiny. Publication of bucchero from Etruscan sites frequently emphasizes the finest specimens, and it is not often pointed out that a certain percentage of bucchero pottery, perhaps even a significant amount, does not fit the description given for the high-end examples. Certainly context makes a difference in the quality and preservation of pottery, often with the specimens from tombs providing the best information about forms and some of the best examples of the fabric. At nonfunerary sites the evidence may provide quite different results. At Gravisca, the port settlement of Tarquinia, Pianu studied a very large sample of broken pottery and was able to make distinctions of fabric, color, and quality, dividing the pastes into six groups.[2] At Cetamura the sample is relatively small, but even so a considerable range of pastes has been noted.

Some twenty-five bucchero vessels have been identified at Cetamura, representing ten or eleven forms, mostly bowls, cups, and chalices for eating and drinking. Only one of these was found in an intact context of the Orientalizing/Archaic period, a fact that is not surprising given the extensive later reworking of the site in Etruscan, Roman, and medieval times.

The one piece of bucchero found in context was part of the packing of a post pit, on the north side of Zone I, suggesting the presence of a timber structure there. Other than that there is minimal evidence for buildings dated to this period, which actually is represented quite well elsewhere in the wider Chianti area, by princely or noble tombs at Castellina in Chianti and Castelnuovo Berardenga (see map 1). At Castellina is the most famous Etruscan monument of Chianti, the tumulus of Montecalvario, boasting four monumental stone hypogea aligned exactly on the compass points, dating ca. 630 BCE.[3] No bucchero was found in the tumulus, but other sites at Castellina have yielded specimens, and in fact bucchero is also known at Poggio La Croce, a hilltop settlement located at Radda, very near Cetamura, as well as at numerous sites near Castelnuovo Berardenga.[4] The handle of a miniature *kyathos* (cup) from Cetamura compares closely with a specimen from Poggio La Croce,[5] and the remains of a *kantharos* (drinking mug; fig. 2.1a) find a close parallel in an elite tomb at Poggione (Castelnuovo Berardenga, end of seventh–early sixth century BCE).[6] A nearly intact saucer (fig. 2.1b), a stamped decoration on a ring-foot vessel (fig. 2.1c), and a bowl with beaked rim (fig. 2.1d) all have comparisons of the sixth century BCE or slightly later from Roselle,[7] which may have been connected with the Chianti through trade along the Ombrone River and Castelnuovo Berardenga (see map 1).

No other pottery that is independently datable to the early period has been found at the site; Greek vases, often imported into Etruria, are missing, and the handmade Archaic impasto commonly found at Etruscan sites does not differ sufficiently from handmade wares at Cetamura of a later period to allow us to be confident of its dating without a clear context.

A Ritual Crevice

As for the fourth-century inhabitants, so far the best evidence for their presence is provided by a deep cut in the sandstone bedrock between Zone I and Zone II (see map 3; fig. 2.2), where quite a large cache of pottery and animal bones was found packed in dark, ashen earth. This material was perhaps ritually deposited because this location was to be the threshold for a gate to Zone I, as attested by remnants of sandstone walls ca. 4.50 meters apart from one another (see fig. 3.6).[8] On top of the packed crevice were numerous fragments of roof tile (fig. 2.3) and evidence of fires set on top of the tiles. The inclusion of neonatal puppies and piglets among the animal remains (along with pig, sheep/goat, and cow) adds to the hypothesis that the deposit was sacred.[9] It is even probable that much of the deposit comes from elsewhere on the site, for example the cleaning of an altar, and that it was a kind of refuse buried mostly at one time. First interpretations of the crevice deposit referred to it as a refuse pit (RP), a

2.2. Ritual crevice in the bedrock between Zone I and Zone II.

2.3. Roof tile used as packing over the ritual crevice.

designation that remains generally valid, with the additional hypothesis that the material is also ritual or sacred in some manner.

The number and variety of vessels for eating and drinking, cooking, and storage (figs. 2.4–2.10) in this large pit, both finer imported wares and everyday ceramics, are considerable and imply the existence of a settled community with outside connections. There are some specimens of Etruscan overpainted ware—including fragments of a "swan cup" of a type coming from Volterra, known at San Martino ai Colli, Poggio La Croce, and numerous other sites[10] and the black-gloss pottery referred to as "Atticizing" (fig. 2.4), actually made in Italy and dated to ca. 350–300 BCE—that help to clarify the date of the deposit.[11] Numerous comparisons exist with materials found in tombs at Grotti, Monteroni d'Arbia, some 10 kilometers south of Siena, dating to the later fourth century BCE. An exceptional piece is a fragmentary oval-shaped platter with a cream-colored slip and geometric designs painted in red over cream.[12]

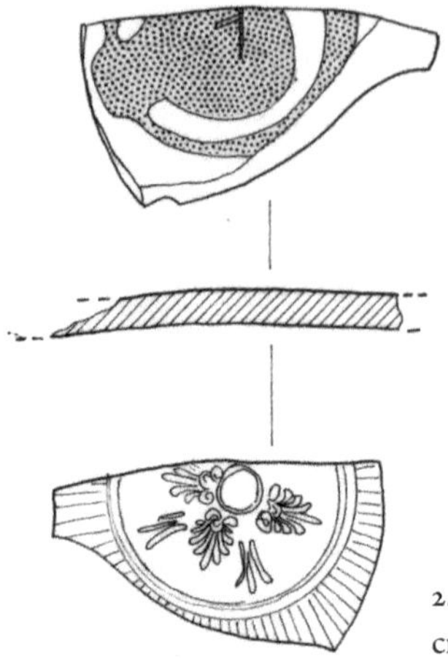

2.4. Black-gloss "Atticizing" ware from the crevice area.

2.5. Rim of large cooking pot (Cetamura Fabric 1) from the crevice.

Some bucchero has been noted both within and on the fringe of the deposit, but it may be residual. The cooking pots include the local ware known as Cetamura Fabric 1 (CF 1; fig. 2.5), and the larger vessels for pouring and storing are represented by Cetamura Fabrics 2 and 3 (CF 2 and CF 3; figs. 2.6–2.7)—all Etruscan fabrics that have a long life at the site (see chapter 3 below).[13] It is therefore quite useful to have these specimens in a well-dated and closed context. In addition there were fine-ware bowls, probably not locally made, of a red-brown and of a gray color, the latter of which often features carination of the wall of the bowl and probably descends from the Archaic ware of gray bucchero (figs. 2.8–2.9).

Some fragments of pottery bear sigla—nonverbal markings of varying usage—that become quite prevalent at Cetamura in late Etruscan times; such marks are found at numerous Etruscan sites of north and south Etruria as well as outside Etruria proper from the eighth century BCE down to at least the second century BCE.[14] A specimen of a ring-foot base in a gray ceramic (fig. 2.10), probably a late adaptation of bucchero, is marked on the bottom with a diagram that divides the rounded field into four quarters (*forma quadrans*). Two of the four fields have individual markings resembling the let-

2.6. Rim of large storage jar (Cetamura Fabric 2) from the crevice.

2.7. Fragment of water jug (Cetamura Fabric 3) from the crevice.

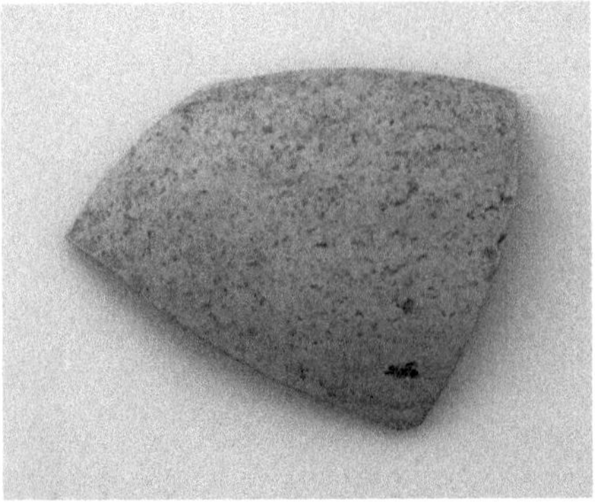

2.8. Red-brown fineware bowl from the crevice.

2.9. Gray fineware bowl from the crevice.

ter *digamma*. Such marks are most likely ritual in purpose. Bagnasco Gianni has noted the presence of this kind of division, with the *forma quadrans* and other siglum forms, at major Etruscan sites such as Caere and has argued that the marks relate to orientation rituals.[15]

One additional ceramic vessel should be mentioned, though its relation to the crevice deposit is not quite clear. At the same level as the covering stratum of tiles was found approximately one-half of a large mortarium lying flat almost directly on the bedrock (figs. 2.11–2.12).[16] The form, featuring a circular bowl with a flanged, overhanging rim intersected by a molded spout, finds its closest comparison in mortaria of a later date. Since the Etruscan gate area was overlain by Roman terracing, it is possible that somehow a later object came to rest on the bedrock. Still, it should be noted that the practice of placing

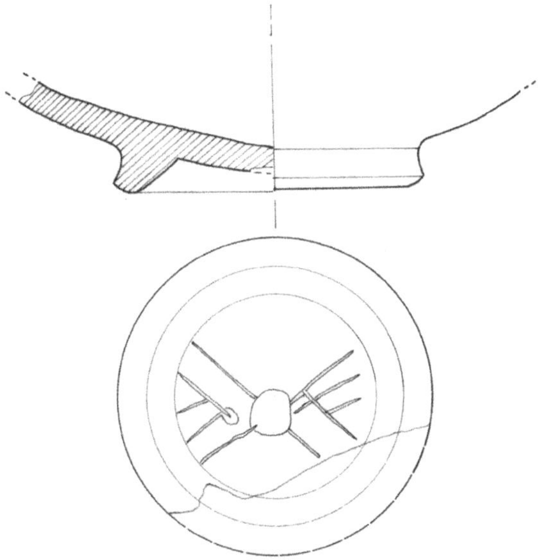

2.10. Gray ware/gray bucchero with siglum from the crevice area.

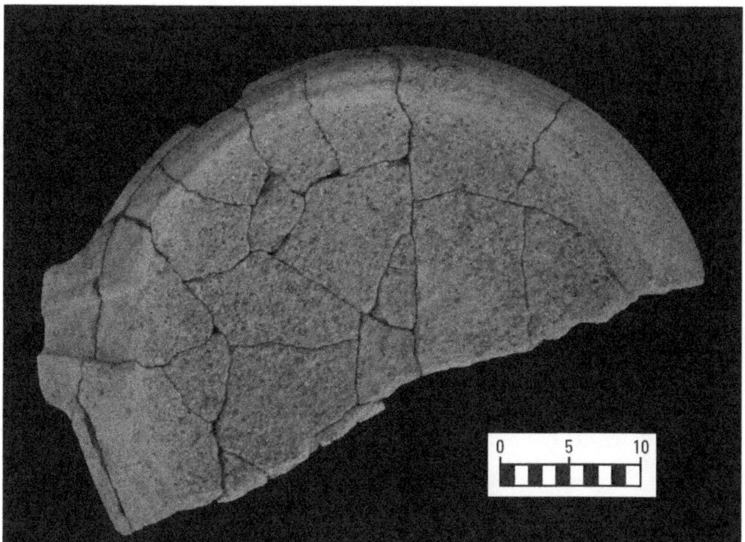

2.11. Mortarium from surface covering beside crevice.

flattened ceramics, especially tile, all around and over the top of the pit was widely observed. The fact that exactly half of the mortarium was deposited also hints at ritual action, as there is abundant evidence at Cetamura of Etruscans halving objects and giving a portion to the gods and retaining a portion for themselves.[17]

Other kinds of artifacts within and immediately around the deposit were rather sparse, e.g., occasional pieces of metal (a small bronze plaque, iron nails, a lead cylinder with a tab of bronze attached), lamps, industrial slag from ceramics and iron, a tiny glass bead, spindle whorls, and various specimens of deer antler, two of which were clearly shaped and used as tools (fig. 2.13). While these do not contribute greatly to efforts at interpreting the society or population of the second half of the fourth century, they do indicate the presence of ironworking and making of textiles, two activities that will become prominent in the next phases of habitation. Apart from the crevice filled with cultural material, thus far there is little indication of any building associated with this group of Etruscans. Soon afterward would appear considerable evidence of religious practices, including a sanctuary, succeeding the sacred activities implied by the ritual crevice.

Etruria farther south was in turmoil at this time, due to what is often referred to as the "Etruscan Wars" between the great Etruscan cities of Caere and Tarquinia and the emerging power of Rome. Probably there was already movement of refugees from these cities to safer territory in the north, a trend that would only accelerate as the Romans continued to push their way into Etruria. Many would be Etruscans, but it is possible that Romans displaced from the countryside were also among the immigrants.

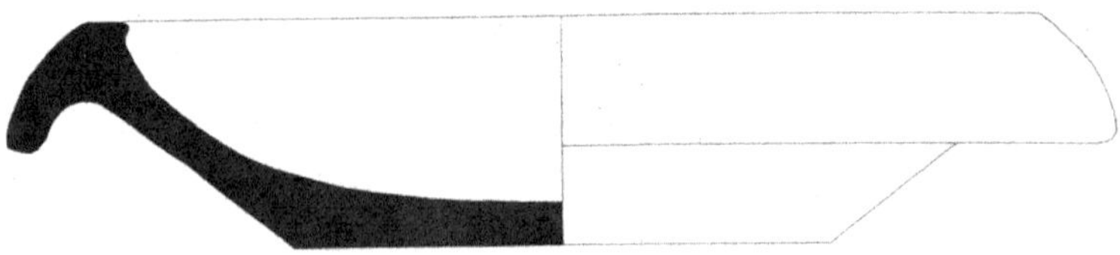

2.12. Mortarium (drawing).

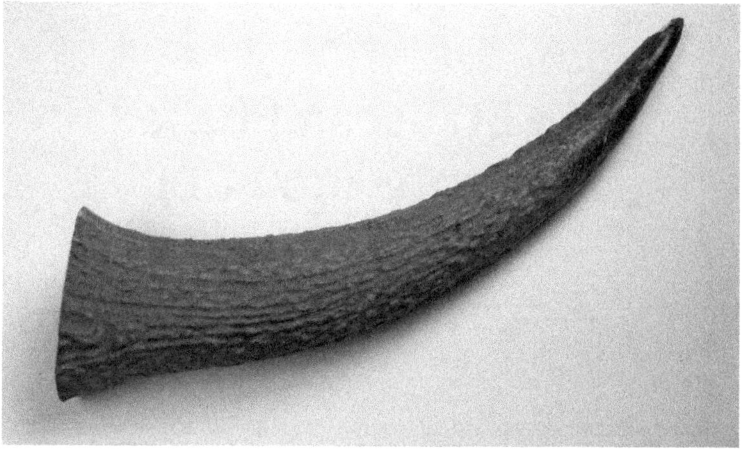

2.13. Deer antler tool from the crevice.

Clues about the society at this time are rare inasmuch as we have no monumental installations apart from what seems to be an entranceway to Zone I. Thus far, no cemeteries or isolated burials are known that may be connected with this period of habitation. The level of culture may be judged mainly by the quality of ceramics found within the crevice deposit, which is relatively high considering that the dining ware is abundant and therefore seems to be of daily usage rather than simply the finest things offered to deities. Comparisons with deposits in contemporary tombs at Monteroni d'Arbia, San Martino ai Colli, and Bosco Le Pici in the Berardenga support the idea that the inhabitants of Cetamura, though not necessarily of elite status, took part in a healthy middle-class level of economy in northern Etruria.[18]

◎ 3 ◎
Late Etruscan Phase I (ca. 300–150 BCE)

A major change occurs at Cetamura near the end of the fourth century BCE. A substantial increase in population is detectable, as there are several major projects that transform the site and that would have required a sizable workforce. Indeed the burial of the materials in the crevice (chapter 2), which seems to date no later than this moment, may have been part of a renovation of the site. The historical context could be linked to a political, social, and military upheaval in general in Etruria[1] but especially at nearby Arretium (Arezzo), where a revolt of the lower classes against the noble and wealthy family (*gens*) of the Cilnii led to intervention by Rome to stabilize the city (302 BCE).[2] The dictator M. Valerius Maximus Corvus brought troops to the area, and the change in control may have given impetus to the departure of members of the lower classes for the countryside. Shortly afterward, in 284 BCE, Arezzo was besieged by the Galli Senones. Roman intervention was at first unsuccessful, but finally the consul M. Curius Dentatus rebuffed the invaders. At the same time there may have been a gradual improvement in the economy of the territory, linked to the calming of tensions in Arezzo and the stronger participation of Romans in the area.

In the wider Mediterranean world, this period is regarded as taking its identity from the spread of Greek culture as a result of the conquests of Alexander the Great and his successors, and accordingly is often referred to as "Hellenistic," that is, "Greekish" or "under Greek influence."[3] In fact at Cetamura, while the site certainly shows connections with other parts of Italy and even the Mediterranean, there is very little evidence of true Hellenizing. A single example of a stamped Greco-Italic amphora of the third century BCE is of considerable interest.[4] It was made by the Latin firm of M. Lurius and was stamped with the name of the artisan, most likely to be read as EUTACHEI, obviously a Greek. E. L. Will noted that the stamp of M. Lurius was one of the earliest of stamps in the Greco-Italic category and that it also occurs in southern France and elsewhere in the Mediterranean.[5] Still, the fact that it is so far unique actually shows how little Cetamura depended on such a connection.

This generalization is based on the habitation site only, since so far no cemeteries or even individual tombs connected to Cetamura have been excavated. It is of course quite possible that imported items were reserved for burials. Unless major new discoveries are made that change the current perspective, it seems prudent to refer to the third to first centuries BCE as "Late Etruscan," building on the identity of the inhabitants as Etruscan rather than as part of a trend that is only vaguely applicable and even misleading in this part of Italy.

Two Wells

Ambitious projects to benefit the community were undertaken in this period on both zones. On Zone I, a well/cistern was dug down into the sandstone bedrock to a depth of 32.43 meters below the ground level (fig. 3.1).[6] It is probably no accident that this depth calculates as exactly 100 Etruscan feet, a figure obtained using the standard foot found at Etruscan Cetamura, of 32–33 centimeters. This well did not obtain its water from an aquifer at the bottom, but rather through seepage from the sandstone walls. It then served as a cistern, the primary purpose of which was to store water as a kind of reservoir. Such a distinction may not have mattered to the Etruscans; in any case, the term "well" is not incorrect, as long as it is made clear that it refers to accumulation of water through the ground and not, for example, from pipes or channels collecting rainwater.

The other well, Structure M on the lower level of Zone II (fig. 3.2),[7]

3.1. Well #1, Zone I.

3.2. Structure M/Well #2, Zone II.

was completely different in construction, although created perhaps only slightly later. In this case, the bedrock was excavated and a layer of impermeable clay was laid upon the rock surface. Within the circle of that layer rose a cylinder of masonry walling, which in turn was packed around with clay. Earth was then filled in all around the clay. The depth of this well was 8.32 meters, which equals 26 Etruscan feet (using a module of 32 centimeters). Similarly, it did not tap into an aquifer. The clay packing around the shaft, which would pose enormous problems to full excavation, must have had gaps that allowed the water to come in at a certain level, for when the well was under excavation the water began to appear at a depth of ca. 6 meters. Thus it, too, must have acquired water through seepage.

Only a few meters north of the well, two walls form an angle (see fig. 4.5) that would have been part of a shelter for storage of huge jars (dolia). Excavations revealed much of the bases of two dolia (A and B) still *in situ*, and the imprint of a third (dolium C) showed where it once stood. Much of the rim (see fig. 3.28) and numerous sherds of dolium A were secured, but it has not yet been possible to create a restoration of the original pot utilizing the thick, heavy sherds. Instead a replica was made using a drawing of the profile of the vessel, made into a 3-D design, and used in a digital router that carved away styrofoam to show the original form of the huge jar (see fig. 3.29).[8]

The Artisans' Quarter

Massive earthworks were undertaken all over on the north side of Zone II, involving scooping out of deep hollows in the bedrock to insert sturdy foundations to create buildings for productive activity.[9] The new buildings, Structures B, C, H, J, K, and N (see maps 3 and 4; E and F have not been dated) have very deep foundations, sometimes as much as 3 meters. The layout of this period produced a north–south orientation of rectangular buildings. In Structure C, the walls were almost certainly made of rammed earth or wattle and daub, because the fill inside the room was a very densely packed, fairly pure, and hard yellow clay that must have come from the collapsed walls.

3.3. Structure K/the kiln.

Researchers are still not certain what the superstructure of the other buildings would have been, but timber is a strong possibility. So far there are no traces of a true fortification wall on Zone II, but the walls of the buildings rising upon these thick stone foundations may have presented a continuous line of faces that would have helped to protect the community.[10]

STRUCTURE K: MAKING BRICK AND TILE

The sandstone foundations of a large kiln—Structure K, for making brick, tile, and loom weights—were laid in the hollowed out area (figs. 3.3–3.5),[11] and pits were left nearby for receiving the debris from the operation of the kiln. Some areas of the deep foundations were backfilled with earth, on top of which were built platforms for the workers to carry out their operations (see figs. 3.15–3.16).

Some of the bricks from the final batch in Structure K were left behind in the kiln, and it is possible to determine something about their usage and nature. Without doubt they were created to go (at

3.4. Structure K/the kiln, showing stone cover applied when the kiln was closed.

3.5. Model of Structure K (by Don Davis).

3.6. View of features on the scarp between Zones I and II. *Foreground*: medieval wall; *center*: fragment of Roman wall; *left*: section of Etruscan gateway.

3.7. Etruscan bricks *in situ* on the scarp between Zones I and II.

least in part) on the scarp in between Zone I and Zone II, because the specimens from the kiln match perfectly with several that were found *in situ* above the ritual crevice. They must have been used in the same episode as the creation of the gateway to Zone I, all of which was later built over in Roman and medieval times (figs. 3.6–3.7). Their firing was carried out in such a way that the core of many bricks was left black, while the exterior was reddened. Laboratory analysis found finely chopped straw within the bricks.[12] An interesting by-product of the industry is the hundreds of fragments of a refractory material that was used to line the kiln and its overhead covering. Several well-preserved examples of refractory bricks show a recurring form (fig. 3.8), roughly rectangular at the base (normally ca. 32–33 cm long, obviously a standard measurement for the forms used), and L-shaped in cross-section. Thus far no parallel is known for the type and its precise usage in the lining of the kiln remains unclear. Some of these bricks were kept for reuse and were found packed into the side walls of Structure K, but this particular shape was evidently not relevant for that usage. Another type of brick made of refractory material was found in the subpartitions of the kiln, forming part of a wall in an upright vertical format. A good example of the "orthostats" thus used measures ca. 11 cm wide and ca. 22 cm high, equaling one-third and two-thirds of the module (fig. 3.9).

3.8. Refractory brick from the workshop of Structure K.

3.9. Refractory brick orthostat from the workshop of Structure K.

The architecture of the kiln features a masonry style typical of the period from 300–150 BCE, in which irregularly shaped stones, unmortared and small enough to be transported easily by one person, were laid in a tidy fashion to create smooth wall faces. The interior plan of the quadrilateral structure is irregular, with the front and back walls measuring 2.61 and 2.62 m on the interior, but the side walls 1.52 and 1.75 m. The thickness of the walls also varies, from 0.50 to 0.62 m. A central partition wall, a *mastio*, made of refractory brick, divides the kiln into two compartments, measuring 0.95 and 0.96 m in width. Subdividers within each compartment, also made of refractory brick, would have helped support some kind of floor for the baking chamber. Beneath that floor was the combustion area, accessed by two stoking channels in the north (front) wall.[13] Remains of carbonized wood within the channels and in the firing chamber were identified as hornbeam (*Carpinus* and *Ostrya*) and beech (*Fagus sylvatica*);[14] the latter is of particular interest because the pieces frequently show holes produced by wood-eating larvae, suggesting that the beech was stockpiled. Beech wood is well known as a material that burns quickly and reaches a very high temperature, and was thus suitable for this Etruscan kiln.

What survives of Structure K is only the lower part of the construction, a situation that is typical for ancient kilns. The nature of the cover or roof can be seen in a model (see fig. 3.5), showing that the walls were corbeled so that the upper part of the kiln would be roughly pyramidal. The cover would have been rebuilt before each firing and then removed when the firing was complete in order to allow access to the finished products. A large-scale reconstruction of Structure K, created by modern artisans at the castle of Spannocchia (near Siena), shows the arrangement; this kiln has been utilized in actual firings of ceramics.[15]

Also found in the kiln were tile, only partially fired, and one irregularly shaped loom weight, imperfectly fired. Numerous fragments of ceramics that were not made in the kiln were also found within it and provide a key to dating it no later than 150 BCE and probably a good bit earlier. Of particular interest were several votive vessels that indicate

3.10. Votive foundation cup from the bottom of Structure K.

3.11. Votive cup from the stoking channel of Structure K.

religious ritual taking place at the kiln. A small cup made of a local unpainted ware, probably CF 3 (fig. 3.10), was found almost perfectly intact at the base of the back wall, and surely must have been an offering at the foundation of the kiln. Another small cup, of a finer quality and painted black, was found partially broken as an offering in the western stoking channel (fig. 3.11). Within the kiln were found fragments of two sacrificial saucers (*paterae*), again with a black glossy surface, scattered all about in pieces in both sides of the combustion chamber (fig. 3.12).

The artisans must have broken and offered these fine vessels to the

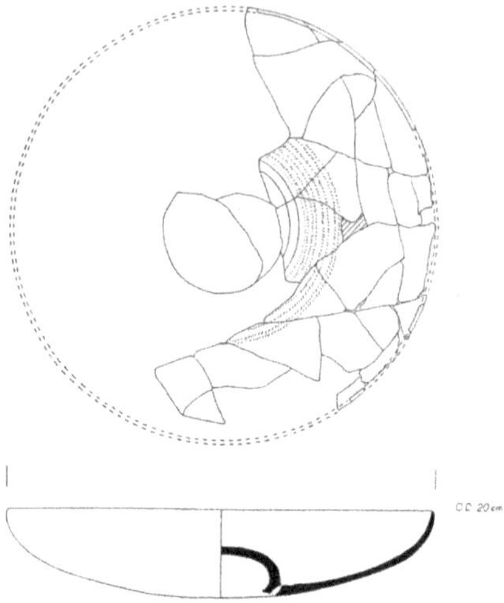

3.12. *Patera* found in fragments in Structure K.

gods, sending up a prayer for the success of the great batch of brick and tile that would be fired. Yet another ritual element was the act of obliterating the kiln when it went out of use sometime in the first half of the second century BCE. As excavation began to reveal the outlines of the kiln, it also brought up evidence of stones placed so as to cover over the structure and confirm that it was out of use. One particularly large sandstone slab covered most of the east side of the structure (fig. 3.4). Thus one of the most striking elements of the Cetamura kiln is the fact that it shows several different kinds of ritual activity—for the foundation of the structure, for the propitiation of the gods during its use, and for the obliteration of the work area.[16] These actions were no doubt carried out on behalf of the artisans themselves, and perhaps also for the community in general. This evidence so far seems to be unique in Etruscan archaeology.

There is so far no known parallel for Structure K in the Chianti area.[17] Indeed not many Etruscan kilns are sufficiently well preserved or published in enough detail to provide comparable information.[18] It is also important that Structure K was probably not the only kiln in the Artisans' Quarter at Cetamura. As discussed below, Structure J may have been the location of two or more kilns.

STRUCTURES B AND C: WATER MANAGEMENT AND TEXTILE PRODUCTION

At the same time that Structure K was created, two rather large rooms, Structures B and C, were constructed to the west. Originally identical in size, these adjoining rectangular structures each measured 15 × 21 Etruscan feet on the interior of the walls (fig. 3.13); a module of ca. 32–33 cm was again used in their creation. The building technique is similar to that of Structure K: a tidy masonry with smooth wall facing. The deep foundations, like those of Structure K, follow a north–south grid of orientation that seems to have been first utilized around 300 BCE and continues to appear on the site. Structure C had a well-paved floor of irregular flagstones (fig. 3.14), a detail relatively rare for Etruscan habitation sites, though well known in tombs. The presence of

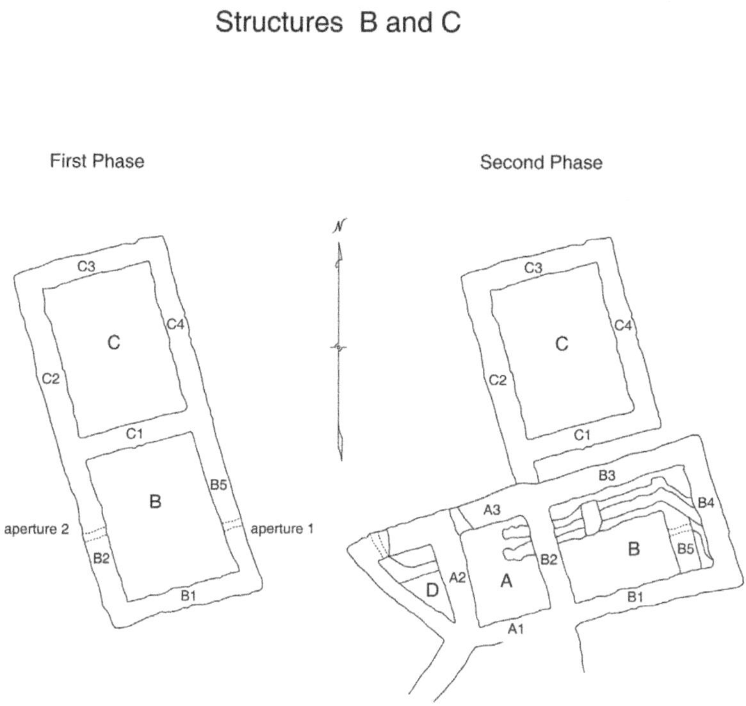

3.13. Reconstruction of building phases of Structures B and C.

3.14. Structure C.

the paving may reflect the usage of Structure C for a particular purpose since within it and around it were found various implements that could have been used in the making of textiles: spindle whorls, spools, weights for the loom as well as grinding stones, possibly for pulverizing dyestuffs.[19] Structure B did not have such a paving, but seems to have served as the basement for a building that would have channeled and collected water. The water would have been useful for the making of ceramics and the dying of cloth, and also for ironworking, which seems to have taken place just to the north of Structure K.

STRUCTURE J: A WORKERS' PLATFORM

In between Structure K and Structure C was Structure J, a long, stone-paved floor or platform that was clearly part of the work yard (figs. 3.15–3.16). The platform was found covered over with ash and carbon as well as numerous by-products of ceramic-making activity. It supported two low stone walls set perpendicular to each other and abutting Structure C to the west, serving as foundations for a small rectangular chamber (fig. 3.16).[20] It, too, was rich in ash deposit and had refractory brick preserved on its east side. A slab of overfired tile rested within it, perhaps a support for firing pottery. This kind of small temporary structure may have been built and rebuilt on the platform

3.15. Structure J, south side.

3.16. Rectangular kiln on Structure J, north side.

over a period of many years. In fact the platform itself seems to have more than one phase, but since excavation has not been completed in the area, the chronological relationship between the various portions remains unclear. A further complication is that the area seems to have been reworked in Roman times.

The platform has some enigmatic features. In various places the pavement was pierced to create lacunae (labeled A, B, and C on map 6). Lacuna A was filled with stones in a roughly circular pattern, basically indicating a break in the paving it was set into. These stones were extracted to reveal an almost sterile yellow earth with traces of ash (fig. 3.17). The best hypothesis, though far from certain, is that this was a depression used for the firing of pottery, with most of the carbon scraped out into the area to the east of it, where in fact there were dense deposits of ash. Also on the east side of lacuna A, excavators found two ritual vessels turned upside down. One—a black-gloss drinking vessel—was pierced neatly with a hole so that a liquid could be poured through the base and into the ground (fig. 3.18).[21] The other, a cooking pot, was found at a level about 25 centimeters higher than the black-gloss bowl. Analysis of the residues in it indicated that it had contained animal fat and wine, perhaps in combination as a stew.[22]

A probe of lacuna B revealed several objects certainly of ritual significance—a stone token incised with letter-like forms and another black-gloss bowl, turned upside down (figs. 3.19–3.20). The base was neatly halved, and much of the rest of the bowl was retrieved. On the interior floor, it bears an abstract siglum.[23] Further evidence of religious offering in the workers' area was found in between Structure J and Structure C: a tiny miniature cup with one handle, broken into three fragments but almost completely whole when restored.[24]

STRUCTURE N: IRONWORKING

Other buildings (Structures H and N) showing the same masonry style and orientation were part of the artisans' zone. Structure N, still under excavation, featured an oval depression in the earth filled with a

3.17. Lacuna A of Structure J.

3.18. Black-gloss votive bowl with perforation, found next to Structure J.

3.19. Inscribed token from lacuna B of Structure J.

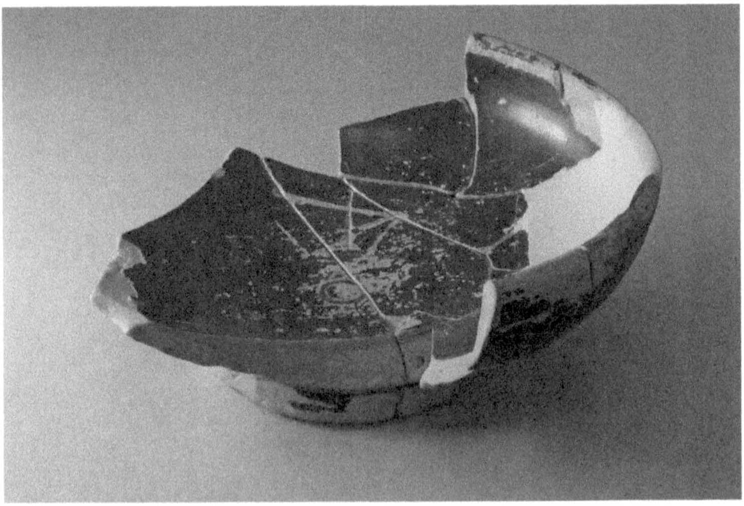

3.20. Votive bowl from lacuna B of Structure J.

3.21. Area of forge in Structure N.

reddish soil, characteristic of a forge workshop (fig. 3.21).[25] Inside the reddish soil was found a single Etruscan black-gloss base, bisected, which was possibly an offering of the same type found in Structure K and along the flank and in lacuna B of Structure J. Within the structure have been found many specimens of iron slag and iron artifacts, mostly unidentifiable and possibly wasters. The ore was certainly not from local sources but probably would have been imported from the well-known deposits at Populonia.[26] Evidence strongly suggests that the ironworkers' area continued in use in Roman times, possibly without a significant break.

Pottery: A Typology

The volume of pottery in and around Structures J and K was enormous. Almost certainly the reason for this was that broken pottery was collected systematically for reuse in the ceramic industry. For one thing there was a constant need for materials to be ground up and made into refractory brick and other linings for the kiln(s). Pottery fragments may have been used as well to create space between pieces that were being fired. Many kiln workshops of the ancient world have yielded "spacers," sometimes made expressly for this purpose and in a particular shape, but so far such items are quite rare at Cetamura. Instead the artisans may have been repurposing sherds of pottery to help separate and brace pieces in the kiln. Structure K contained inside of it a good bit of broken pottery that otherwise is hard to explain. (It definitely was not being made in this brick kiln.)[27]

The result is that within the finds from this general area we can study the gamut of pottery of the Late Etruscan period at Cetamura, even though the vessels are almost always fragmentary. The principal types are the imported wares painted black or red, and the local wares, unpainted, that served for cooking, storage, and drinking and dining. These are summarized in the following sections.

PAINTED WARES

Black Gloss (ca. 350–first century BCE)

This is a well-known fine ware, often decorated with incised or striated lines or with floral designs such as the lotus or palmette (fig. 3.22). It was very popular for all kinds of dinnerware, such as plates, bowls, and cups, but also for miniature vases offered to the gods. The interior paste is a light orange, pink, or buff, and the surfaces are covered with a glossy black paint. It was imported from various areas, but in particular Volterra and Arezzo.[28]

Red Gloss (ca. 250/200–100 BCE)

At Cetamura, this ware is found almost exclusively in bowls of the size used for soup or porridge, occasionally decorated with a stamp on the floor of the interior (fig. 3.23).[29] The red paint is thin and glossy when new, but is prone to become dull and flake off, exposing the light pink interior. The bowl type is known at Volterra from ca. 250 BCE and is sometimes referred to as "Volterran presigillata," something of a misnomer, since *sigillata* means "stamped" and "pre" sigillata ought

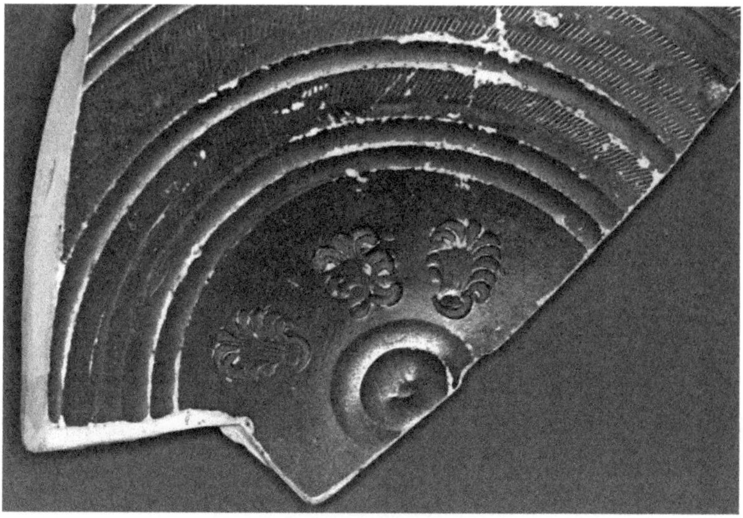

3.22. Black-gloss pottery with lotus and palmette stamps.

3.23. Red-gloss bowl of Volterran presigillata with star stamp.

to mean before a practice of stamping began. Further, recent studies have shown that the ware may have been made at other sites besides Volterra. Repeatedly there is evidence that the ware came to Cetamura well after usage began at Volterra, probably no earlier than ca. 150 BCE.[30]

UNPAINTED WARES: "CETAMURA FABRICS"

These wares are extremely common at Cetamura, appearing as early as the fourth century and as late as the first century BCE. Because they tend to change little through the centuries, they are hard to date from the paste or the form alone, and one must rely on context. Originally referred to as "utilitarian pottery," they are so frequent at Cetamura that they have been recognized as "Cetamura Fabrics," though in fact they occur generally in the Chianti area.[31] Comparanda will be noted for the several categories.

Cetamura Fabric 1 (CF 1; fig. 3.24; see also fig. 2.5)

This is a cookware of a muddy orange color and a thick, coarse paste, sometimes made on the wheel and sometimes handmade. It often has large white inclusions of calcite or limestone. During cooking these inclusions sometimes fell out, leaving vacuoles in the ceramic. The pots are sometimes blackened on the inside from the cooking oil and/or on the outside from fire.[32]

Cetamura Fabric 2 (CF 2; fig. 3.25; see also fig. 2.6)

CF 2 pottery is of varying thickness, bright orange or dull orange with red or brown sandstone inclusions of varying shades and sizes. CF 2 was used for storage vessels, loom weights, roof tiles, and various other objects.[33]

3.24. Example of Cetamura Fabric 1.

3.25. Example of Cetamura Fabric 2.

Cetamura Fabric 3 (CF 3; fig. 3.26; see also fig. 2.7)

CF 3 vessels are white, pink, or beige with a rough, sandy exterior. The fabric in cross-section has a gray interior. This is the most popular of all wares at Cetamura and is one of the most distinctive. CF 3 was employed for tableware and for vessels used for mixing, pouring, and storing. Many examples of hydrias (water jugs) were found near the water sources and kiln on Zone II; the tableware is generally thinner and more delicate than the other types of vessels. Open forms are not known.[34]

Cetamura Fabric 4 (CF 4; fig. 3.27)

CF 4 is a very refined orange or buff ware with white or colorless grains and small glistening particles (mica). It is close to CF 2 but does not have the red/brown sandstone inclusions. Sometimes the interior of the cross-section is gray. Used for dining and for votive cups, CF 4 is often thinner and more elegant in its vessel shapes than CF 2.[35]

DOLIA

Numerous fragments of dolia of varying sizes have been found around the site. Occasionally portions have been found *in situ*, such as the bases of two quite large specimens (dolium A [figs. 3.28, 3.29] and dolium B; see fig. 4.17 for another example) located near Structure M, probably dating to the late fourth or early third century BCE. Evidence was found for a third dolium in the area, C, when the impression of it was discovered in the same beaten earth level in which dolia A and B were seated (see map 5).

The fabric is normally very dense, with temper of calcareous material, mica, and black sandstone. Often the rim and parts of the surface are coated with a smoothing slip. These huge vessels, with very thick walls and a large rim, were used for storage of items in bulk, probably liquids such as oil.[36] The completion of excavation of two walls that sheltered the storage area (see fig. 4.5) helped to determine

3.26. Example of Cetamura Fabric 3.

3.27. Example of Cetamura Fabric 4.

3.28. Rim sherd from dolium A.

3.29. Reconstruction of dolium A in styrofoam.

the dating of the area, when ceramics of the same horizon as the crevice between Zones I and II were found in the lowest levels of the earth fill. They were in use from around the beginning of the third century BCE and down into the middle of the second century. More will be said about the area where they were found below.

Artifacts in the Artisans' Quarter

INSCRIPTIONS AND SIGLA

Many examples of what is traditionally referred to as graffiti ("scratched or incised marks") have been found at Cetamura, particularly in the Artisans' Quarter. Among these are inscriptions on black gloss with the names of two of the gods of Cetamura, Lur and Lein(th) (figs. 3.30–3.31),[37] written from right to left as is most typical of Etruscan writing. These Etruscan deities are not very well known and have no counterpart in Greece or Rome, but, given the evidence from cult activities at Cetamura, they were probably gods of fate and fortune, consulted through divination.[38] The word *aes . . .* , Etruscan for "god(s)," also occurs on a black-gloss bowl.[39] Further, there are inscriptions with the names of individuals such as Lausini on a Volterran red-gloss bowl[40] and Cluntni on a small CF 4 votive cup,[41] also written from right to left (figs. 3.32–3.33). These are most likely the names of Etruscan men who inhabited or visited Cetamura and made offerings to the gods with their own names inscribed.

We noted earlier a related category of marking—the "siglum" (pl. "sigla"), a nonverbal sign or symbol found especially on pottery but occasionally on other objects, such as loom weights.[42] Most of these marks seem to have been made after the firing of the ceramics (figs. 3.34–3.35) and are especially conspicuous on black-gloss vessels when the incision cuts through the color coat. Among the sigla incised after firing on pottery, the five-pointed star (*pentaculum*, fig. 3.34) occurs several times at Cetamura. Other abstract signs are the "dry branch" (*ramus siccus*), the "double axe" (*bipennis*; see fig. 3.27), and the "radiating lines" (*lineae radiantes*, fig. 3.35). These are all sigla that occur

3.30. Black-gloss fragment, inscribed with the name of Lur.

3.31. Black-gloss fragment, inscribed with the name of Leinth.

3.32. Red-gloss bowl of Volterran presigillata, with inscription *lausini*.

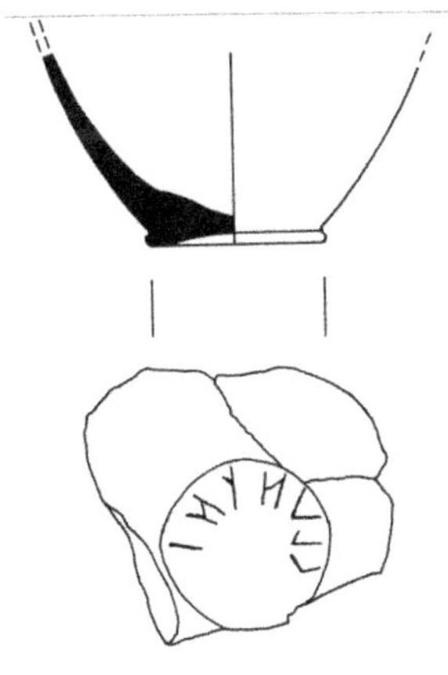

3.33. CF 4 votive cup, with inscription *cluntni*.

at other Etruscan sites, and the implication is that they constitute a kind of vocabulary that was understood widely. There are also sigla in the form of a single letter (*A* and *X* are the most popular) and in the form of a number. Etruscan numerals are the predecessors of Roman numerals, and on the whole resemble them, though the Etruscan numerals are normally written from right to left.

The sigla on loom weights often were made during production and were created sometimes by a punch or by finger swipes.[43] These are not properly called "graffiti" since they were not scratched onto the surface. They are often abstract signs such as a cross-mark that divides

3.34. Black-gloss pottery with siglum: *pentaculum.*

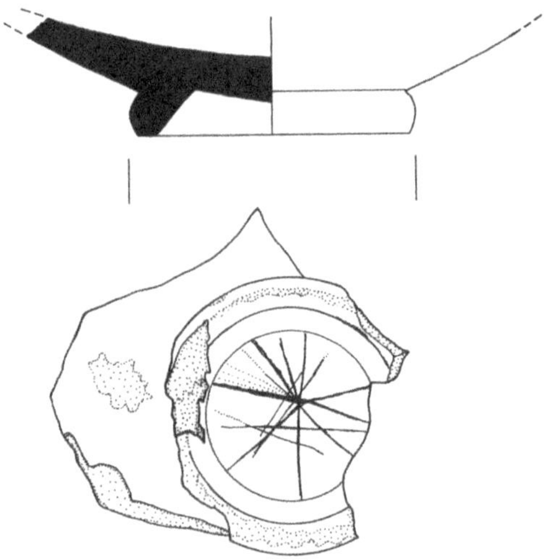

3.35. Black-gloss pottery with siglum: *lineae radiantes.*

the field into four areas (*forma quadrans*; fig. 3.36), or a circle, diamond, or oval shape.

Thousands of objects bearing sigla have been found on Etruscan sites.[44] Some two hundred sigla are known from Cetamura, mostly of the third–second centuries BCE, utilizing a range of alphabetiform, numeriform, and abstract signs. Their meaning is far from clear, but it is probable that there is no one single explanation for all of them.

3.36. Ceramic loom weight with siglum: *forma quadrans*.

The marks on loom weights, made before firing, may be there to indicate which craftsmen made the weights or could be intended to help identify weights as belonging to one particular weaver. The sigla in the form of letters could be abbreviations of someone's name, but this theory does not explain why the letters *A* and *X* are the most frequent. Sigla in numerical form could be used in calculations. For example, the handles of pitchers often have numbers on them, which may be there to indicate the quantity the pitcher would hold.

GEMS AND GAMING PIECES

From inside Structure H comes an Etruscan gem made from red cornelian (fig. 3.37), carved with a relief of a scarab on one side and an intaglio cut into the gem in negative on the other side.[45] Stylistically it belongs with the Etruscan gems carved in the style called *a glo-*

3.37. Cornelian gem with intaglio carving of hero and dog.

bolo, in which the main lines are punctuated by globe-shaped cuts,[46] and may date as early as the fourth century BCE. An *a globolo* gem of similar date (much damaged) was found at Poggio La Croce and another, well preserved and closely resembling the Cetamura scarab, was found at Castiglion Fiorentino near Arezzo.[47] The location of the workshop(s) that made these *a globolo* gems is not known.

The scene shows a powerful naked male baiting a dog as he holds a rope to catch the creature. The dog could be the underworld guardian Kerberos (though he has only one head), and the hero then would be Hercle, the popular Etruscan counterpart of the Greek hero Herakles. Often Etruscan narratives of myth show such variants from the Greek stories, but the story may instead be something purely Etruscan.

There is no reason to believe that the scarab gem was carved at Cetamura itself, but it should not be ruled out that community artisans were making or dealing in jewelry. Two carved ring stones found in the second-century sanctuary display a local style of carving, and a gold earring (found in a nondiagnostic context) and a bronze earring (possibly votive) add to the inventory of valuables.

On Zone II have been found several vitreous discs shaped like ring stones, with a flat bottom and a rounded upper surface.[48] Two are made of an opaque black glass and one is colorless. Such objects sometimes served as gaming pieces, and the same may be said for several small polished stones made of green serpentine that come from the area. While the pieces may have been intended for usage in actual games, there is also evidence that such items were offered to the gods as tokens for good fortune.[49]

This is perhaps the best place to note that a number of pieces of flint stone have been found at Cetamura, particularly on Zone II in the area of the sanctuary and the Artisans' Quarter.[50] The flint is of good quality, with medium to fine grain and color ranging from gray to black and red. Some pieces are clearly worked as tools (projectile point, scraper), while others are cores or debitage from the making of tools. When datable the items seem to belong to the Upper Paleolithic, ca. 20,000–10,000 years before the present, a period that finds little representation in the Chianti-Valdarno region. The large number of pieces of debitage would suggest the existence of a tool-working station on the site, but so far there is no evidence of a Paleolithic habitation horizon at Cetamura. It may be that these are collected objects, brought to the site by the Etruscans. The flint would have been quite useful in starting fires in the kiln area and on the altars of the sanctuary.

COINS AND METALS

Apart from coins found associated with the well on Zone I (see below, fig. 5.5), the area that has yielded the most coins at Cetamura is the Artisans' Quarter (fig. 3.38). The coins range widely in date, from the third to the first century BCE, including an Etruscan bronze coin of unknown origin, with a god in wolfskin cap on the obverse and a leaping dog on the reverse (see fig. 4.7);[51] several Roman bronze *asses* featuring a head of Janus and a ship's prow; a silver quinarius of the moneyer Quintus Titus; and a silver quinarius of Mark Antony and Lepidus with religious paraphernalia on both obverse and reverse.[52] The reason for the abundance of coins in this area may be the provi-

3.38. Coins found in the Artisans' Quarter. *Top row* (from left to right): silver quinarius of Mark Antony and Lepidus, 43–36 BCE, obv. ritual elements; bronze coin of Kos, 167–88 BCE, obv. head of Herakles; unidentified bronze coin. *Bottom row*: unidentified bronze coin; halved Roman *as*, third–second century BCE; unidentified bronze coin.

sion for the sale in currency of some of the products of the artisans' zone, and these coins could thus represent some of their earnings. So far, no dedicated marketing area has been identified, but there are unexcavated stretches of level land to the southeast of the artisans' zone that would have been appropriate for such.

Far and away the most abundant metal in the area is iron. The forge area in Structure N has already been mentioned (see fig. 3.21), with its numerous examples of slag and possibly discarded iron artifacts. There were also numerous nails discovered in the artisans' area, all made of iron, but some hemispherical bronze studs were found that must have served as caps for nails. More will be said about metals below in the discussion of Phase II and the creation of the Etruscan Sanctuary in Building L.

Fauna and Flora

Study of the biological remains from Well #1 for the first phase of the Late Period (ca. 300–150 BCE) relates to the lowest parts of the well, where an abundance of water-logged wood has been found, indicating a significant presence of deciduous oak and cherry trees on the site. Also found were numerous waterlogged specimens of worked wood of many varieties: oak, elm, beech, hornbeam, and walnut (see fig. 5.2).[53] Pollen studies are compatible with these findings, and also indicate in Well Group I, ca. 300–200 BCE, an abundance of wild grasses and the growing of cereals (oat and wheat, and barley and einkorn).[54] Boar and deer were exploited, and pig, cow, and sheep/goat were raised.[55]

Most important of all is the evidence for vineyards, especially the presence of grape pips, many of them cultivated rather than wild.[56] Pilot studies to analyze the DNA and provide carbon dating have shown the likelihood that grapes were already present in the fourth century BCE. One specimen showed an identical genetic makeup with a specimen found in Well #2, a remarkable result considering that these two grape seeds are dated almost six hundred years apart, through carbon 14 analysis of companion seeds in each locus (ca. 300 BCE and ca. 300 CE, respectively). Several other seeds of other dates in the two wells had identical genetic markers.[57] The evidence indicates that there was a long, consistent history of cultivation of the same kind of vine. So far most of the evidence suggests that the berries of these grapes grown in Chianti were white. But research is only beginning and thousands more seeds await analysis.[58]

Conclusion

Late Etruscan Phase I at Cetamura seems to have been a time of relative calm and surprising stability for the inhabitants. As noted at the beginning of the chapter, this period is generally referred to as "Hellenistic," calling to mind the turmoil of the times of Alexander and his competing rival generals as they carved out their new kingdoms in the East. For Cetamura, there is no evidence for difficult times, even though it is during this period that the Romans had their wars with Carthage, and Hannibal even marched through some of the most fertile fields of Tuscany on his way to the devastating defeat of the Romans in the Battle of Lake Trasimene (217 BCE).

The larger Etruscan cities were indeed affected, as we know from the fact that Arretium (Arezzo) was used as a base by the Roman consul Flaminius. Arretium was later enrolled to help the Roman war effort by equipping ships for Scipio Africanus (205 BCE) against Hannibal, contributing massive amounts of bronze weapons: three thousand shields and three thousand helmets, fifty thousand javelins, short spears, and lances; axes, shovels, sickles, baskets, and hand mills to furnish forty war ships; and one hundred and twenty thousand pecks of wheat (Livy 28.45.16). The richness of the contribution strongly suggests that Arretium was prospering and strong after the troubled times around 302 when there had been a class rebellion.

On the fringe of Arezzo, Cetamura may have partaken of the relative calm and prosperity of the third century in northern Etruria, even during the time of the march of Hannibal. In fact none of the Arretine products for the war effort would have been produced at Cetamura, except possibly implements made of iron. It seems that the community carried on life as usual while Rome was struggling to grow into the role of a pan-Mediterranean power.

4
Late Etruscan Phase II (ca. 150–75/50 BCE)

A new throng of settlers appears to have come to Cetamura sometime around 150 BCE or a little later. This is around the time of the building and coming into use of a major Roman consular road, the Via Cassia, theorized by some to have been constructed in 154 BCE.[1] This important highway from Rome went through southern Etruria and, following preexisting Etruscan roads, ran past Clusium and Arretium up toward Faesulae (Fiesole), the Etruscan city dominating the Arno River in the area where Florence would later be built. This corridor would no doubt have made a significant difference in communication, trade, and agriculture for the Etruscans of Cetamura. Cetamura pollen samples from Well Group III of Well #1 (ca. 150–100 BCE) suggest increased anthropogenic activity in this period, with a reduction in oak pollen and a notable amount of cereal pollen.

Structures A, B, and D (Maps 3–5)

In this period many changes were made in the structures of the Artisans' Quarter, and a different style of masonry appeared.[2] The walls were still created without mortar, but the stones are often huge, certainly too big to be managed by a single person (figs. 4.1–4.3). They are roughly shaped, and when inserted into the wall often protrude rather than present a smooth face. Some walls are one meter or more in width. Tool marks occur frequently, in particular the drill holes made to receive a wooden or metal wedge inserted to split the stones (fig. 4.3).

4.1. Structure B, looking west.

4.2. Structure B, looking east.

4.3. Structure B, tool marks.

This type of masonry was used in an ambitious reworking of Structure B. The east wall was partially dismantled and new, thicker walls were built on the east and the north; these were spliced into the Phase I walls on the west and south. The massive basement could have supported a very tall and imposing building, probably of two stories or more.

The interior of the thick, deep foundations of the new Structure B had a covered stone channel running through it, taking water to the west, where a new building was created, Structure A (fig. 4.4). Here the Phase II masonry style became even more distinct, with highly irregular stacks of sandstone capped by large flattish slabs jutting into the interior or outward to the exterior. This construction also must have been a basement, but probably also would have served as a cistern. The south side had only a few courses of stone, beneath which was the huge scooped out pit in the bedrock, which could have held water effectively. On the north side, a curious positioning of the stones on the top created what looks like a doorway threshold, but the sides of it seem to taper and grow too close together for a person to pass through (fig. 4.4). This is plausibly identified as a channel through which the water could overflow if it reached the top of the cistern.

To the west of Structure A was a third construction, Structure D (see maps 3–5),[3] the date and purpose of which are elusive. The triangular foundations show Phase II masonry on the party wall with Structure A and on the north wall of Structure D. A rough channel was created at the base of the party wall so that water from the cistern in Structure A could drain into Structure D. The north wall as it stands is very interesting, since it preserves the effect of stone stairs leading down to a water retrieval area, which in turn was pierced by a drain that carried water off down the hillside. These two walls seem to indicate that Structure D was built at the same time as Structures A and B, Phase II, thus ca. 150 BCE–75 BCE. The triangular construction would have served for further catchment of water. But when one looks at the wall on the western "leg" of the triangle, contradictions arise. Here the wall is made of the tidy masonry typical of Phase I. Excavations on the south and west of the leg have shown that the masonry style is

4.4. Structure A, looking north.

similar to that of Phase I but with the occasional integration of fragments of flat tiles into the wall (fig. 4.5). The wall rests on bedrock, and pottery found in the lowest fill stratum dates to the end of the fourth century BCE. The conclusion is inevitable. This wall was built around 300 BCE, and it must have been left standing when Structures A and D were first built and Structure B was reworked. Further examination of the area appears below, where Building L is discussed.

Other changes took place at Cetamura at the beginning of Late Etruscan Phase II. Structure K went out of use, as we may deduce from fragmentary pottery found in a sealed context within the kiln. A thorough review of the ceramics found no examples of Volterran red-gloss presigillata or gray ware, both of which are typical of Phase II. The datable forms are mainly black-gloss vessels of the third century BCE. What is interesting is that debris in the pits outside the kiln did contain a stratum of material from Phase II, showing that in the Artisans' Quarter the practices of gathering and recycling pottery continued. Very likely one or more new kilns would have been constructed, since normally where an Etruscan kiln workshop is discovered, there will have been multiple kilns over a period of time.[4]

4.5. Dolia area with wall of Structure D on the left.

Lacuna A and the rectangular kiln on Structure J may have continued in use, but there is no firm stratigraphy to confirm this conjecture.

When Structure K ceased to be used, the workers' space seems to have been reconfigured. A gap in masonry between Structure C and Structure H was filled in with Phase II masonry (see map 4). It is possible that this gap between the two structures had allowed air to be pulled into the kiln area, and it was no longer needed at this spot.

Artifacts from Structures A and B

Thousands of artifacts came out of Structures A and B. Those from B are not easily datable according to stratigraphy, since the building had two phases and water seems to have circulated through the deposits. In addition materials may have washed down into the building from the slope above after it went out of use. Structure A, as a building of Phase II, yielded a clearer chronology of items from the later second century BCE, but it, too, may have received washed-down materials. Some of the items from these contexts have already been mentioned, such as the inscriptions and sigla (see figs. 3.32–3.33, 3.35). Some ten

4.6. Romano-Campanian coin from Structure B. 270–240 BCE. Obv. head of Apollo; rev. human-headed bull and Victory. Drawing by Tina Ross after de Grummond 2000: pl. LII.a.

4.7. Etruscan coin from Structure B. Third century BCE. Obv. head of a god with wolfskin cap; rev. prancing dog. Drawing by Tina Ross after de Grummond 2000: pl. LII.b.

coins were found in the two structures, all dating to the third or second century BCE. Of particular interest are a Romano-Campanian coin of ca. 270–240 BCE and an Etruscan *litra* of the third century BCE (figs. 4.6–4.7), both from Structure B.[5]

The deposits were rich and varied, embracing many examples of all the Cetamura fabrics, Volterran presigillata, and abundant black gloss (figs. 4.8–4.9). The deposits of black gloss were especially dense in Structure A, with many specimens datable to the second century

4.8. Reconstruction by 3-D printing of black-gloss pyxis from Structure B.

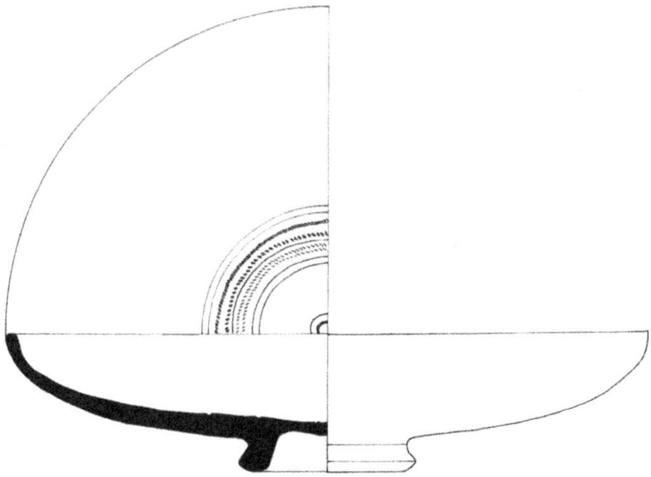

4.9. Black-gloss plate from Structure A.

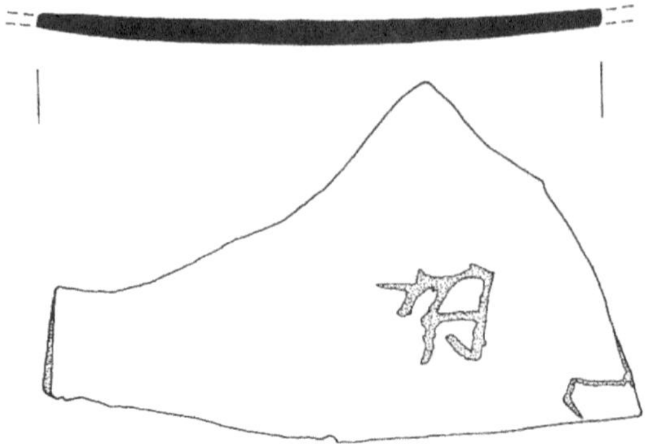

4.10. Black-gloss sherd with inscription ALP(?).

BCE.[6] Sigla were quite numerous, and of particular interest were examples with the ligature of three letters: *alpha, lambda,* and *pi* (fig. 4.10).[7] So far this ligature has been identified in eleven examples coming from Structures A, D, and L and other contexts; it occurs on local wares, especially for cooking, as well as internal red-slip ware (a cooking vessel) and on black-gloss pottery. They are almost certainly ritual sigla, most likely indicating dedication to a god, but the intended order of the letters is uncertain. The identification of the name of the god depends on the order in which the characters are read: ALP could refer to Alpan, an Etruscan goddess of good will; APL could refer to Aplu, an Etruscan variant of Apollo; and LAP could refer to Lapse, an epithet or byname of a god found at the sanctuary of the Etruscan god Suri at Pyrgi.[8] Bagnasco Gianni, leaning toward the reading of Alpan, noted that the siglum had immediate visual impact even for those who might not know what the ligature stood for.[9]

Building L: The Sanctuary of the Etruscan Artisans

Structure L on Zone II is the principal component of what may be called the Sanctuary of the Etruscan Artisans.[10] There can be no doubt that the artisans who occupied the workshops adjacent to the sanctuary had an awareness of and relationship with the sacred area, creating objects that were offered there, perhaps sometimes by their clients, sometimes by the artisans themselves. Such objects as nails and other items made of iron; weaving implements such as loom weights, spindle whorls, and spools; miniature bricks; polished stones and carved gems and rings—all of these may be hypothesized to be connected with the local artisans.

Building L (also referred to during excavation and on maps as Structure L; fig. 4.11 and map 5) was a trapezoidal structure, with an interior courtyard open to the sky on the southeast, within which were contained a ritual cavity in the bedrock and a central rustic altar (Altar 1). The location of the sanctuary, on a hilltop removed from any urban connections, means that it should be categorized as a "rural" sanctuary, closely connected to elements of nature and not particularly easy to access.[11] In plan it is an unusual Etruscan structure, having some features that compare in a suggestive way with Etruscan temples but in other ways resemble the sacred precinct area that sometimes stretches in front of a temple.[12] One may also compare certain ritual precincts not connected with a temple. The trapezoidal plan[13] features two diverging foundation walls or wings on the southwest and northeast; the better preserved southwest wall is ca.

4.11. View of the Sanctuary of the Etruscan Artisans.

22 meters long and 1 meter or more in width. On the southeast is a short wall, ca. 9 meters. The foundations of the wings run on a diagonal to the grid used in Phase I and do not line up with the compass points. They draw closer together toward the southeast. The southeast section of the enclosure is interpreted as a courtyard open to the sky, where smoke from the sacrificial fires on the main altar and a subsidiary altar—Votive Feature 2, or, as it came to be called, Altar 2—would have an easy outlet.

There are foundations of a single, small room (Room 1) on the southwestern wing, measuring 2.85 × 0.84 m, which was excavated down to bedrock with very few finds emerging. Did it perhaps feature a wooden stairway that would allow access to an upper floor or gallery? On the northeast side of the plan is a suite of chambers, Rooms 2–5, that are oriented according to the principal compass points and in this way are basically aligned with the buildings of the Artisans' Quarter as first laid out in Phase I (see map 3). Rooms 2 and 3 are close in size to Room 1 and the other rooms are somewhat larger. The masonry style of several walls has been analyzed as belonging to Phase I, but reused in the new sanctuary. Very little has been found in the rooms to provide clues for their usage or date when they were created.

From the configuration of the courtyard as thus far revealed in the latest excavations and as seen in varying detail on the map by Alvaro Tracchi (see map 2), it is possible to argue that the main entranceway into the sanctuary was on the narrow end on the southeast. There may have been a separate entrance into Room 3, where a gap in the foundation wall may mean there was a door. Elsewhere around Building L, there is no evidence for an entrance. The northwestern sector of the building, organized with reference to the diagonal of the southwest wing, remains enigmatic. North of Altar 1, two possible rooms are suggested by walls meeting at right angles, though these are poorly preserved and the full plan of the rooms cannot be ascertained. A stone platform or paving also on the north adjoins the cistern (Structure A) and features a line of large stones that runs parallel to the south wall of the cistern, while another line of stones runs perpendicular to the wing wall. In general the stone platform seems to be encircled by large stones, with smaller stones in the interior, an arrangement similar to that of Altar 1, discussed below. It is not possible to determine if this pavement was within what would have been a small room, or whether it was exposed to the elements. Tracchi suggested this feature might be a base for a tower.[14]

The foundations of the wings of Building L are built of large irregular blocks of sandstone often showing conspicuous tool marks. These are the diagnostic characteristics of Late Etruscan Phase II, as seen in Structures A and B, dated ca. 150–75 BCE (see fig. 4.3). Normally, the foundations do not go deep into the soil. A dramatic exception to the way the walls of the sanctuary are built is found in the northernmost stretch of wall, adjacent to the dolia A, B, and C, forming an angle with the western wall of Structure D (see fig. 4.5). This wall also rests on bedrock, with a fill around its base of the late fourth century BCE. Although constructed in a style that is not as refined as that of the western wall of Structure D, nevertheless it predates that wall, which seems to have been built to act as a buttress for this very heavy wall. The current interpretation of this arrangement is that these two taller walls (ca. 2.30 m high) were built to protect the area where the dolia were placed for storage. Both probably existed before Building L, but the wall on the south must have been reworked to be included as part of the sanctuary. This area seems to have gone out of use at the end of Late Etruscan Phase I or beginning of Late Etruscan Phase II. An enormous amount of debris from the kiln area was dumped in here, in effect covering over what was left of dolium A and dolium B.

For the superstructure of Building L there is no evidence. The walls may have been of timber or rammed earth, while the floor of the courtyard and some other areas of the sanctuary feature a beaten earth floor of a fine, yellow-to-golden sandy clay, with occasional intrusions of rock or carbon. On the west side of the courtyard and all the way up to and around Altar 1, this beaten earth floor was found to be almost completely sterile. On the east side were concentrated six of the seven votive features known so far.

The orientation of Building L is intriguing, since it seems to have faced south, a common direction for the front of an Etruscan temple.[15]

Information about orientation and the gods worshiped is rare, and thus it is quite significant that this building at Cetamura, oriented to the east of south, may be connected with the worship of the gods Lur and Leinth.[16]

Very likely this orientation had to do with setting up a sacred space for augury, with both the south and the east as favorable regions. It is tempting to compare the courtyard at Cetamura with the deep front porch of a typical Etruscan temple, the part referred to by Vitruvius as the *pars antica,* the "part in the fore" (*De architectura* 4.6.6). The *pars postica,* the "part behind," would be the cella-like Rooms 2 and 3 as well as other structural elements of the northern side of the complex interior. But since the overall ground plan is by no means shaped like a normal Etruscan temple structure, it is not necessary to pursue further the famous Vitruvian description. It is interesting to note, however, that the concept originally implied in the Latin word *templum,* as a delineated area for the well-known Etruscan practice of augury, may be quite applicable here.

This augury could have taken place from Altar 1, an irregular tetragonal platform of large, roughly cut stones of Phase II, running partly perpendicular to the southwest wing wall.[17] The platform of the altar measures 2.46 m (southeast side) × 1.32 m (northeast) × 1.94 m (northwest) × 1.85 m (west). The largest stones are placed on the perimeter while in the center of the altar are smaller stones. One large stone projecting from the northeast corner features an unusual deep scoop in the upper surface which seems more than incidental and which could have been a focal point for pouring liquids. No diagnostic artifacts were found in the earth around Altar 1, but it is hypothesized to belong to Phase II on the basis of the masonry style.

As far as ritual is concerned, the cavity immediately to the southeast of the main altar may have been of the greatest significance (see map 5; fig. 4.12). It is a depression with a diameter of approximately 50 cm and a maximum depth of about 20–25 cm. Inside the cavity is a protrusion, interpreted as a part of the bedrock shaped to look like something emerging from the cavity. A channel in the bedrock, with a slight gradient, leads down to the cavity from the northwest, i.e., from

4.12. Central cavity in the sanctuary.

the area of Altar 1 (the connection with the altar is not fully clarified), and a similar channel leads from the southwest down to the cavity. Liquid offerings could have been poured from either direction.

The cavity, the channels, and the ridge along one side of the channel were found beneath a thick layer of earth fill, featuring pebbles and a dense, sandy clay. Over this fill was then spread the beaten earth of the courtyard belonging to the later second century. In other words, at this point we can hypothesize that the cavity was in use during Phase I of Building L, and in Phase II was intentionally and carefully closed over, probably ritually. Much of the pebble fill remains to be extracted, but what has been excavated is sterile and no artifacts have been found within the cavity or the channels. With excavation complete on the southwest side of Building L, no votive features have been identified. Instead, these have all been found on the northeast side of the channels and the cavity, suggesting that there may have been some way of marking the location of the cavity even after it was filled in.

The depression or cavity with its strange protuberance must have had something to do with the original designation of the spot as sacred. Other Etruscan sanctuaries with a similar cavity have often been connected with oracular or prophetic activity, and it may be hypothesized that such was the case here.[18] The gods may have been revered and consulted for what they could reveal about fortune, fate, and good luck, always a concern in the ancient world. Evidence from the excavation of Well #1 confirms the presence of an oracular cult at Cetamura, as will be discussed below.

Votive Features of Building L

In the course of excavation of the sanctuary, some seven votive areas ("Features") were identified (see map 5).[19]

Votive Feature 1 (VF 1), the first to be discovered, was also the most important. It probably was a foundation deposit for Building L. Here, a pit sunk into the ground adjacent to a party wall of the sanctuary (measurements ca. 1.13 × 0.90 m; depth ca. 0.50 m) contained three levels of offerings with some fifty items, probably all deposited in the same ritual act, suggesting that a group was present for the inauguration (fig. 4.13). The offerings were broken, burned, and buried in a ceremony that most likely went on for several hours. Though the ritual itself would have been elaborate, the offerings were mostly of a modest nature—unpainted miniature cups (fig. 4.14), a pitcher (fig. 4.15), a large but thin-walled storage jar (fig. 4.16), and a dolium (heavy storage jar) that contained numerous grapes, apples (or pears), and unidentified flowers (fig. 4.17). Grains (barley, emmer) were also found in the pit, but no animal bones were found in VF 1 or in any of the other votive features associated with Building L.

Objects of metal included a number of nails of different shapes and sizes, two of them strategically placed to indicate the east and west

4.13. Votive Feature 1 under excavation.

4.14. Miniature cups from Votive Feature 1.

4.15. Pitcher from Votive Feature 1.

4.16. Thin-walled storage jar from Votive Feature 1.

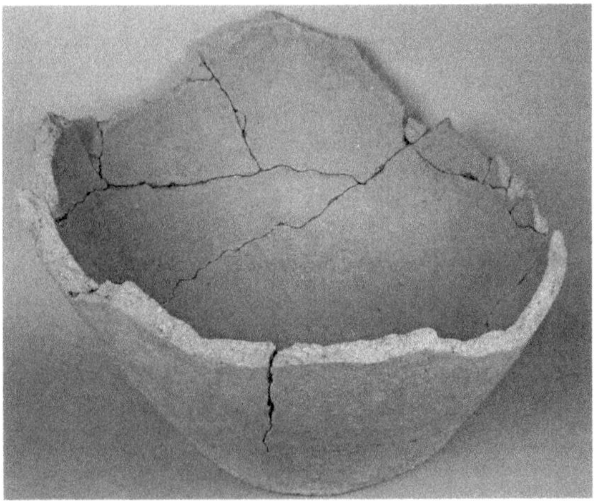

4.17. Dolium from Votive Feature 1.

compass points, while the north and south points were marked by two separated fragments of a handle coming from an impasto jar of a type not seen elsewhere at Cetamura. The identification of the nails as cult objects, most likely created by the ironworkers and perhaps their particular offerings, is verified by their presence in other votive features.[20] An interesting grouping was presented on the east side of the pit, where a large iron nail or spike was found together with an iron ring set with a gem carved with an abstract design (or two birds?); nearby was a single coin, a very important find that serves to date the deposit and confirm the chronology long suspected for the walls of Building L. It is a Roman denarius (fig. 4.18) of a type struck to commemorate the founding of the Roman colony of Narbo ca. 118 BCE, referencing the names of the founders Lucius Licinius Crassus and Gnaeus Domitius Ahenobarbus. The coin is of bronze clad with silver, with serrated edges. Though of modest value monetarily, it provides a striking *terminus post quem* for the ritual of VF 1, which is consistent with the single piece of precisely datable pottery found in the pit, a black-gloss saucer of the second half of the second century BCE.[21]

Votive Feature 2 (also labeled subsequently as Altar 2) is of a very different nature (fig. 4.19). Rather than a pit, it is better described as an in-ground hearth or altar made of sandstone rubble (ca. 1.30 × 0.80 m), a rustic type of altar attested at other Etruscan sites and in literary references.[22] A number of offerings, in this case no doubt made by individuals, were still lying on the altar amid the charcoal from the sacrificial fires: a bronze Roman *as* with obverse head of Janus, iron nails, a halved spool, a halved loom weight, a miniature brick, a polished stone—in short, all modest items that could have been offered by the artisans. The charcoal included wood from oak, beech, hornbeam, and hop-hornbeam.

In the other votive features was evidence of several striking rituals: VF 6 was an amphora rim separated from its vessel, turned upside down and set in the ground as a focal point for the pouring of libations. VF 7 contained a segment of a pot filled with cooked chickpeas set next to a halved wine goblet, meant as a hearty meal for the gods; around that offering were the cut-up pieces of an iron strigil and of an iron shaft perhaps belonging to a candelabrum. The metals offered continued to represent the low end of the economic scale, including more iron nails and an ovoid lead weight in VF 4. Other vegetal offerings were found in the same area as the votive features, including olives, grapes, and barley, and the kinds of wood used to burn the sacrificial fires were oak (both evergreen and deciduous), hazel, and elm.

There is little evidence on Zone II of continued Etruscan activity

4.18. Silver clad denarius of Lucius Licinius Crassus and Gnaeus Domitius Ahenobarbus, from Votive Feature 1. Ca. 118 BCE. Obv. head of Roma (damaged); rev. Gaul in chariot. Drawing by Tina Ross after de Grummond, Giachetti, and Marosi 2009: pl. 4.16.

4.19. Votive Feature 2 (Altar 2).

after this period. A conspicuous stratum of burning was observed in Structures A, B, and C, belonging to sometime in Late Etruscan Phase II,[23] but precise archaeological indicators are few. Further, as will be seen in the discussion of Well #1, there are many artifacts that can be dated comfortably to the period of ca. 100–50 BCE on Zone I. Possibly only Zone II was abandoned in the early first century BCE. This was the period of the Roman Social Wars (91–88 BCE) and Civil Wars, which engulfed Etruria and seem to have had a devastating impact on many Etruscan settlements.[24] The Roman generals Marius and Sulla marched and countermarched through Etruria. Of particular relevance for Cetamura were Sulla's vicious siege of Volterra (82–80 BCE) and, around the same time, his destruction of Faesulae (Fiesole) to the north. Subsequently, according to literary evidence, the city was colonized by Sulla's veterans, with considerable unrest among the local populace. It was a very difficult time.

◉ 5 ◉

The Wells of Cetamura

FROM ETRUSCAN TO ROMAN

The two wells on Zone I and Zone II at Cetamura have yielded an enormous amount of information. This material makes it possible for us to track the activities of daily life on the site as well as the economy, the environment, agriculture, and religious activity during the Etruscan period, beginning around 300 BCE and running until the Late Roman Empire, ca. 300/400 CE.[1]

Well #2 (Structure M), on Zone II

Structure M has been named Well #2 because it was the second well to be excavated at Cetamura. It seems to have been constructed around 300 BCE, but was cleaned out and reused during the Late Roman Empire, and thus the main evidence it provides for the Etruscans lies in the architecture itself, described above (chapter 3). With its tidy masonry of the type used in Late Etruscan Phase I, it seems to be contemporary with the kiln, Structure K, with Structures C, H, and N, and perhaps at least a part of Structure D. Two of the walls of Structure B, reused in Phase II, were already in place at this time, presumably with the other two walls of this phase. A few walls of Structure L, which were reused and integrated into the later sanctuary, suggest that there may have already been a sacred structure at this time, which may have been centered on the cavity in the bedrock (see map 5). It thus seems likely that M originated to provide water for an early phase of the artisans' community and sanctuary.

5.1. Bronze statuette of a female figure from Well #2.

Numerous fragments of hydrias (water jars) made of CF 3 have been found around the kiln, no doubt once used to retrieve water from Structure M. It is also likely that there were religious activities associated with the well, though due to the cleaning episode very few ritual items have been found. A significant exception is an Etruscan rustic bronze figurine of a female making an offering, excavated from the well at a nondiagnostic level but probably dating to the third or second century BCE (fig. 5.1). It is a fairly common type in northern Etruria, grouped under "Mass production of the third cent. BCE" by M. Bentz.[2] The stylized elongated woman (or goddess?) wears a high-waisted Hellenistic tunic with a mantle draped over it. The missing proper right hand would have held a *patera* (saucer) for pouring a libation. The tang at the bottom indicates that the statue was inserted upright into some kind of base, probably made of stone. Presumably later it fell or was discarded in the well, or just possibly was cast in as an offering.

Well #1, on Zone I

From Well #1 emerged thousands of artifacts along with organic evidence for the nature of the environment in the Late Etruscan period. Items were retrieved from this well in thin stratigraphic layers ("loci," sing. "locus") of ca. 10–25 cm that were subsequently grouped on the basis of datable objects such as coins, pottery stamps, and characteristically Etruscan or Roman artifacts. These in turn may be linked with cultural phases on the site as known from excavations outside of the well and as discussed previously in this volume. Table 5.1 presents the well groups beginning from the bottom of the well, where the locus numbers were the highest, as they were the strata that were dug last. Thus the strata can be read developmentally in groups. Well Group I is thus the oldest material, of Late Etruscan Phase I, and the final stratum, Well Group VIII, encompasses the latest material, of the Late Roman and medieval periods.

The amount of organic material preserved in the waters was staggering, especially as concerns wood.[3] From Well #1 alone hundreds of water-soaked pieces have been recovered. They represent a wide variety of characteristics—burnt and not burnt, worked and unworked. Taking into account the results of pollen studies in combi-

Table 5.1. Chronology of Well #1, from bottom to top levels

Cultural Phase	*Date Range*	*Locus/Loci*	*Well Group*
Late Etruscan Phase I	ca. 300–200 BCE	112–108	I
Late Etruscan Phase I	ca. 200–150 BCE	107–105	II
Late Etruscan Phase II	ca. 150–100 BCE	104–100	III
Late Etruscan Phase II *and* Late Roman Republic (Transitional Etruscan–Roman)	ca. 100–50 BCE	99–95	IV
Late Roman Republic	ca. 50–30 BCE	94	V
Early Roman Empire (Augustus to Tiberius)	ca. 30 BCE–37 CE	93–92	VI
Early Roman Empire (Caligula to Nero)	ca. 37–68 CE	91–83	VII
Later Imperial Roman *and* Medieval	ca. 68 CE–1200 CE	82–1	VIII

5.2. Wooden knob from Well #1.

nation with actual pieces of wood that have been examined, some sixteen different taxa of trees are known to have existed at Etruscan Cetamura: one softwood: *Abies alba* Mill. (silver fir); and fifteen hardwoods: *Acer* sp. (maple), *Buxus sempervirens* L. (boxwood), *Carpinus betulus* L. (hornbeam), *Cornus mas* L. (Cornelian cherry), *Corylus avellana* L. (hazel), *Euonymus europaeus* L. (spindle tree), *Fagus sylvatica* L. (beech), *Fraxinus* sp. (ash), *Juglans regia* L. (walnut), *Ostrya carpinifolia* L. (hop hornbeam), *Pinus* (pine), *Quercus* sp. *caducifolia* (deciduous oak), *Quercus cerris* (turkey oak), *Quercus ilex* (holly oak), and *Ulmus* cf. *minor* (elm).[4]

The lowest level, Well Group I, contained the highest concentration of worked wooden objects,[5] including a large beam (oak) of unknown usage, a spool or pulley (hornbeam) probably once connected with a system for buckets, and a number of fragments of a single wooden bucket (beech). Also extracted were a perfectly preserved wooden knob (wood unidentifiable; from furniture? fig. 5.2) and a spatula-shaped instrument (walnut) with traces of scorching on the rounded end that perhaps indicate it had been used in cooking. The only artifacts in the well that were not made of hardwood were from silver fir. Particularly interesting were several small, thin rectangular items from Well Group IV, best described as tablets, which may have been used in divination.[6] Comparanda from other sites and from literary evidence indicate that silver fir was often used for writing tablets. Plautus mentions *sortes* (lots) made of fir that were thrown into water (*Casina* 384) while Cicero describes *sortes* at Praeneste that were made of oak (*De divinatione* 2.41.85). Colonna has published *tavolette* from the well west of Temple B at Pyrgi, dating to the third century BCE, that were found to be made of *Abies alba* Mill.[7]

Similar tablets of oak and hornbeam were found in numerous loci, from the bottom of Well #1 all the way up to Roman times. It has not yet been possible to examine these tablets for the presence of writing, since the majority of the Cetamura wood has not been processed and dried.

Various dating indicators are provided by the artifacts in Well #1. These must often be queried as to whether the artifact was an older object that was deposited as an offering at a later date or, on the other hand, whether it may be an object of a later date that managed to trickle down into a lower level. The latter case would be especially relevant for coins and other small objects. Another kind of problem results from the probability that there were episodes of dumping from time to time, and this has been reflected especially in Well Group III, as will be discussed below.

Datable black-gloss pottery from Well Group I and carbon 14 dating provide the basis for the hypothesis that Well #1 was first used near the end of the fourth century or the beginning of the third century BCE. Thus it may well have been part of the massive overhaul of the site evident in Zone II, and may be quite contemporary with Well #2, even though the two shafts are completely different in construction.[8] Another hypothesis, very difficult to test, is that the well had been dug in the fourth century but was cleaned out for reuse at the beginning of Late Etruscan Phase I, around 300 BCE.

Soon afterward we see the first evidence that the water source was

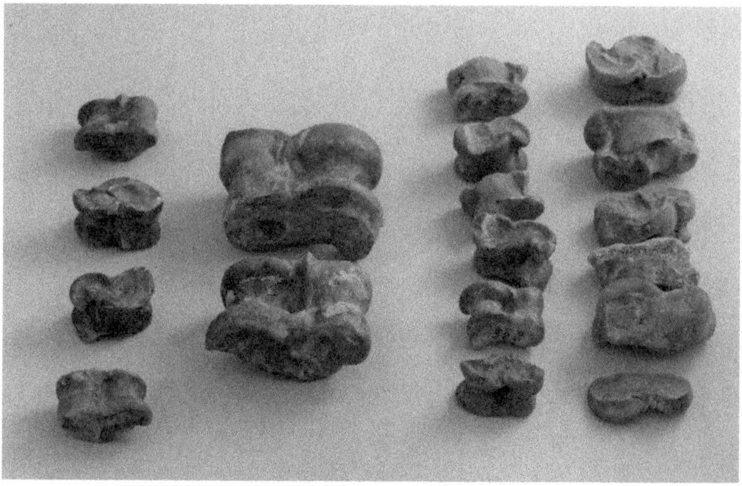

5.3. Astragali ("knucklebones") from Well #1.

treated as sacred and that religious rituals were performed there. For an Etruscan well to have such a status is not at all surprising, since in antiquity water sources were normally considered sacred.[9] A variety of ritual items have been found, comprising ceramic and stone "gaming pieces." In reality these were tokens of good fortune or divination (see fig. 5.13); four-sided astragali (fig. 5.3) ("knucklebones," actually from the ankles of animals), thrown and used in the same manner as dice and found at numerous sacred sites of the Mediterranean world; miniature votive cups; and an interesting assemblage of ring-foot bases from black-gloss bowls and cups that seem to have been deliberately chipped into a shape that could be inverted and used as a little cup with the ring-foot repurposed as a rim (figs. 3.26, 5.4).

Coins were also offered in the well:[10] thirteen specimens were found in the Etruscan and Transitional levels (the lowest in locus 103, Well Group III, 150–100 BCE), mainly Roman Republican bronze *asses*. Also discovered in Well Group III was a Greek coin probably struck by Hieron II, tyrant of Syracuse, ca. 265 BCE, closely imitating contemporary coinage of Ptolemy II of Egypt, with obverse, head of Zeus Ammon (?) and reverse, eagle with a partially preserved inscription of the Greek word *basileus* ("king"). Helping to date Well

5.4. Inverted ring-foot base used as a cup, from Well #1.

Group IV, the transitional loci, was a silver denarius of Lucius Rubrius Dossenos (87 BCE; fig. 5.5).

As noted above, Well Group III seems to have been subject to a quite heavy dumping episode. It is impossible to do justice to the amount of finds from these very rich loci. Most abundant of all were fragments of the local ware CF 3 (of a light cream, yellow, or pink color and a gritty texture), used for the table and for storage. The most common forms thus far seem to be pitchers and hydrias, that is, vessels that would have been used regularly to draw water from the well, but the sherds were in such quantity and in such a worn condition that it seems likely they had been broken outside the well and were accumulated in a heap that was then discarded into it. A remarkable find was an amphora for table use, completely intact, of a fabric not customary at Cetamura (fig. 5.6). Immediately above it was a segment of a bronze handle, probably from a bucket, with a terminal in the shape of a bud (fig. 5.7). A piece probably belonging with this handle,

A

B

5.5. Silver denarius of Lucius Rubrius Dossenus from Well #1. 87 BCE. Obv. head of Minerva; rev. triumphal chariot.

5.6. Domestic amphora from Well #1.

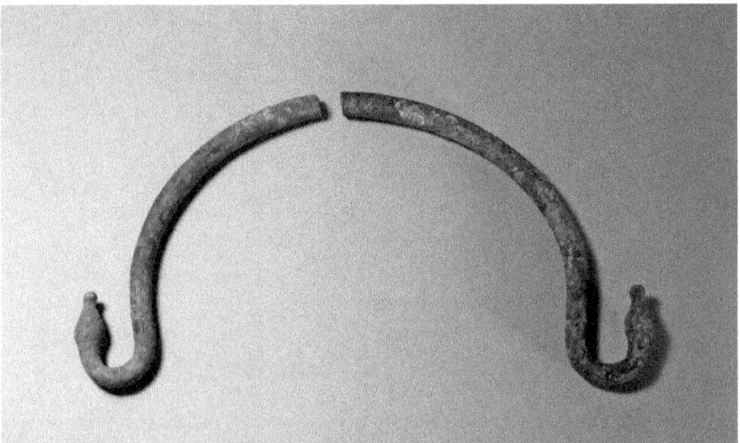

5.7. Bronze handle of a situla from Well #1.

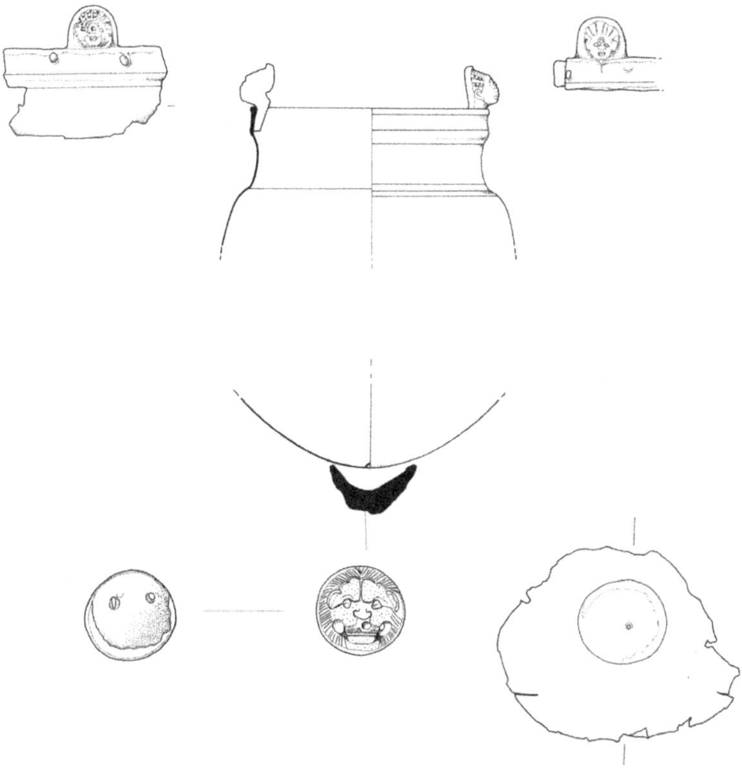

5.8. Situla M (drawing).

though not joining perfectly, was found in locus 98, in Well Group IV, described below.

Among the special objects in Well Group III were two bronze Etruscan situlae (buckets), situla M in 104 and situla L in 102 (figs. 5.8–5.10, 5.11–5.12).[11] Situla M (fig. 5.8) is of a type with an ovoid body that may be dated to the later fourth or the third century BCE, known to have been used by women as part of their grooming equipment;[12] this type of situla did not sit upon a surface but was kept suspended from its handle. The Cetamura example, with body severely damaged, was decorated with a feline head on the bottom (fig. 5.9) and African heads on the handle attachments (fig. 5.10). Situla L is a type of stamnoid bucket used in wine service, incised with a running wave pattern

5.9. Situla M: feline terminal.

5.10. Situla M: African heads.

and a guilloche, with images of a Skylla-type monster for the handle attachments (figs. 5.11–5.12). The Skylla figure and the general decoration of situla L, with incised patterns of guilloche and wave, show connections with works from Populonia,[13] which may be the source of this object. It, too had seriously deteriorated, but it is possible to reconstruct almost the whole profile from the remnants that remain. It also dates to the fourth century BCE, raising, along with situla M,

5.11. Situla L.

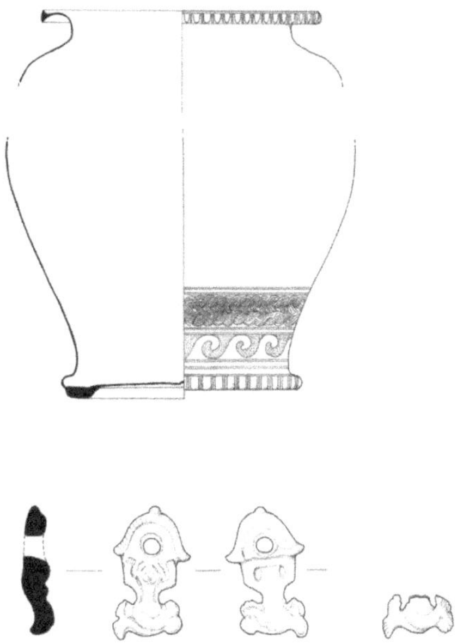

5.12. Situla L (drawing).

the question of whether these fine objects belonged to some earlier deposit on the surface (a sacred area?) and thus ended up in a level of the second century BCE, or whether they were still in use and actually were employed to get water from the well at this date. Etruscan mirrors of the late fourth or early third century BCE depict the same types of buckets as Cetamura situla L and M being used beside a well.[14]

Numerous items are certainly evidence of ritual in or around the well. Some 54 votive vessels, mainly miniatures,[15] and 46 ceramic and stone tokens in different shapes, some halved,[16] all suggest a practice of making offerings, perhaps with divinatory aims (fig. 5.13). An astonishing array of astragali[17] was found in these loci: 71 from sheep/goat; 27 from pig; 1 from a wild boar; and 4 from roe deer (see fig. 5.3). Among the other finds from loci 104–100 were two intact weights of the truncated pyramidal type as well as fragments of seven others.[18] The lowest were in locus 104. The deposition of such weights in the well was also probably a ritual act, as a total of 42 were eventually found. Some weights bear stamps (fig. 5.14) or sigla on the top (see fig. 3.36); one intact weight made of lead in the shape of a truncated pyramid (412 g) was found in Well Group IV, corresponding to the period of transition from Etruscan to Roman.

Most of the above-mentioned weights would have been for use in weaving, one of the main artisanal occupations at Cetamura. Other crafts are represented by a wide range of materials. Obviously used as tools were five specimens of hard, flat, smooth sandstone, of the right size to fit into the hand of an adult; one of these even seems to have been fitted with a handle made of deer antler. Several specimens of sawn deer antler prongs would have been useful as punch tools. Well over one thousand items of iron were found, for the most part rusted and disintegrating, including wrought objects and discards as well as scoria from smelting. Many of these surely would have been thrown in intentionally as offerings of value for their metal, like the offerings in the votive features on Zone II. The slag, extremely common in the Artisans' Quarter, probably indicates trade relations with Populonia, the main source for ore and greatest center for ironworking in all of Etruria. Among the identifiable utilitarian objects were iron attach-

5.13. Tokens of divination from Well #1.

5.14. Loom weight with griffin stamp from Well #1.

ments for buckets and iron chains, also part of the water retrieval system. No doubt some of the objects were tools, but these are now unrecognizable due to their very poor condition.

In the transitional group (Well Group IV) can be detected a distinct upswing in more valuable objects and materials, some of which could possibly be linked with the hypothesized dumping episode associated with Well Group III, while others could be regarded as showing an increase in contacts with Romans. From locus 97 came a bronze handle of an Etruscan wine strainer of a type known from the late fourth and third centuries BCE (fig. 5.15) as well as a fragment of a bronze axe head, also possibly of a (considerably) earlier date. A bronze rod was found in locus 96 (fig. 5.16). It is clearly a measuring implement, as can be seen from the series of carefully spaced notches in the bronze and from its pointed end, which would have served well as a punch. It is stamped with an artisan's name in Latin, PHILEM. . . . Six worked bone implements of a kind identified alternately as either hairpin or stylus for writing were included in this group (fig. 5.17).

One-of-a-kind objects included an oval-shaped glass paste gem set in an iron support (perhaps a ring), with an intaglio image of the drunken Hercules urinating, as well as an ivory die, a carved bone pendant of a phallus (fig. 5.18), and a disc of cast blue glass appropriate for a ring stone. Perhaps most telling was a small polished stone of a serpentine-like material (Italian *oficalce*), inscribed in Latin on both sides (fig. 5.19). Preliminary results suggest that the inscription is a dedication, by a Roman perhaps from Arretium. That the well continued to receive ritual offerings is also confirmed by dozens of objects found in these loci: 38 votive cups, 20 tokens (none later than locus 97, however), and astragali—45 of sheep/goat and 7 of pig, representing a slight diminishing from the numbers in Well Group III. It is interesting that wood was almost completely absent.

Typical of the period is the significant increase in items that are of higher monetary value and that show a blending of Etruscan and Roman cultures, to such an extent that sometimes we would not be able to say easily which culture they belonged to. Obviously the ob-

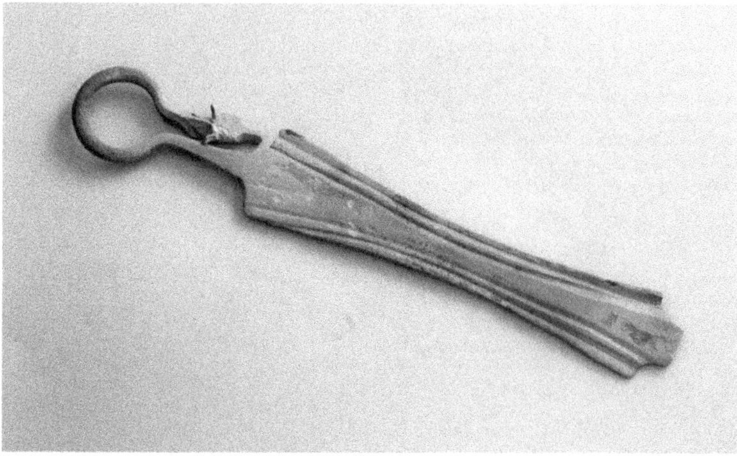

5.15. Bronze handle of a strainer from Well #1.

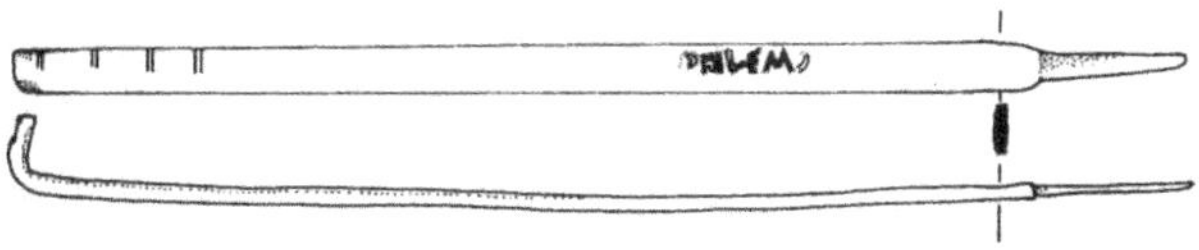

5.16. Bronze tool with inscription PHILEM . . . from Well #1.

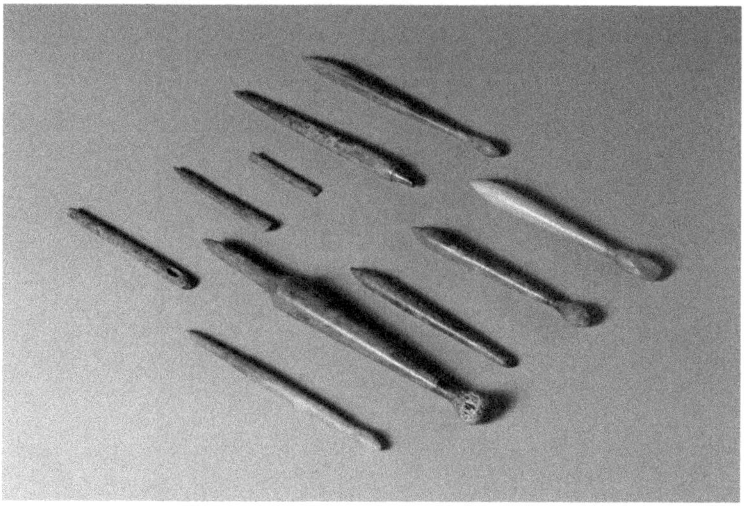

5.17. Bone implements (styli or hairpins) from Well #1.

5.18. Bone phallus amulet from Well #1.

5.19. Polished stone with Latin inscription from Well #1.

jects that are present in the "transitional period" with Latin writing on them have a Roman origin. On the other hand, Latin inscriptions need not indicate that items were not meant for use by the Etruscans. It is interesting that the bronze measuring tool with the Greek name Philem(us) stamped on it is exactly the type of object an Etruscan artisan might make his own. Further, there are many Roman coins from Cetamura that belong to the Late Etruscan phases, but it is not necessary to see their usage as indicating the presence of Romans. Though some Etruscan cities did strike coins and there is at least one Etruscan coin from Cetamura, the standard strong currency comprised Roman bronzes and silver of the later Republic.

Excavations collected a substantial amount of pollen[19] and seeds from the first four well groups.[20] This material supported the evidence from wood about the forest of Chianti at this time, and it revealed some of the foods consumed, e.g., hazel nuts, olives, and grains. Of particular significance in these groups and also the later ones were the numerous well-preserved water-logged grape seeds, around 450 specimens, some wild but many more cultivated, that have provided extended evidence of the importance of vineyards at Cetamura in Etruscan and Roman times. The faunal remains included boar and deer but also indicated exploitation of pig, sheep/goat, and cow[21] and the presence of birds such as pigeon (especially), barn owl, small owl, sparrow, swan, and woodcock.[22]

6

Roman Cetamura (ca. 50 BCE to Late Antiquity)

The two wells at Cetamura shed much light on the cultural transition from Etruscan to Roman at Cetamura. While there is some evidence, in itself not surprising, of increasing contact with Romans in the period of Well Groups III and IV (ca. 150–50 BCE), it is not until Well Group V (ca. 50–30 BCE) that there is a clear indication that Roman inhabitants had actually settled at Cetamura.

The pottery gives the first evidence, by means of a fragment of a red-gloss platter (*terra sigillata*) with a stamp of the firm of C. Septimius, which operated in central Italy ca. 40–20 BCE; this is the earliest of some fourteen stamps on Roman *terra sigillata* found in Well #1.[1] Within the same group were found characteristic artifacts such as a well-preserved squared brick (20 × 20 × 4 cm) of the type used in a Roman under-floor (hypocaust) heating system and fragments of Roman glass such as had not appeared before.

Also within Well Group V was found a bucket of a type different from either of the Etruscan ones (situlas L and M, see figs. 5.8–5.12). Situla K (fig. 6.1) is very well preserved except that the disc of the base had become separated from the bucket.[2] It belongs to the classification known as the "Kurd" type, a simple and rugged form the dating of which ranges from as early as the seventh century BCE to the period of the Roman Empire. Thus situla K cannot be dated other than by its place in the shaft of Well #1, but it is certainly different in form and bronze content from all of the buckets found in Roman loci above it (e.g., fig. 6.8), and the possibility that it is Etruscan should not be ruled out.

6.1. Situla K.

The Settlement of a Roman Veteran

Some years ago, excavations on Zone I produced evidence of Roman baths with a hypocaust system, hypothesized to date to the period of Augustus (fig. 6.2).[3] These previous results tend to find confirmation in the stratigraphy of the well. A rather more striking recent discovery provides even greater clarity for the overall picture. In a fissure in the bedrock on Zone I was discovered a small unpainted jar roughly teardrop shaped, but with a flat bottom, deposited upside down (fig. 6.3). The narrow neck appeared to be chipped. Removal of the earth from the neck revealed that the vessel had been used as a repository of silver denarii and quinarii, the latest of which dates to exactly the moment when Octavian/Augustus dismissed his troops after the defeat of Antony and Cleopatra at the sea battle of Actium in 31 BCE (fig.

6.2. View of baths, Zone I.

6.3. Repository vessel for coins.

6.4).[4] The collection of coins includes specimens of the naval fleet coinage of Antony (fig. 6.5), presumably seized by Augustus and used to pay his veterans at dismissal, and one coin with obverse head of Antony and reverse head of Cleopatra. Similar coin deposits in Italy and elsewhere dating to the time Octavian consolidated his power, ca. 29–27 BCE, and before he took the name of Augustus, seem to illustrate the same phenomenon of a veteran who received his pay and his land.

Baths and Production

It seems then, that right around 29–27 BCE, the land at Cetamura was assigned to a veteran who buried his demobilization bonus and began to develop his holding by building a small Roman bath on Zone I in what has been called Area G (see map 7). Unfortunately most of the Roman-age buildings of Cetamura were dismantled later, during the Middle Ages, and only a few of the posts of the hypocaust system were found *in situ*. On Zone II, it appears that the new owner tried to continue to exploit the artisans' area, since there is evidence of continuity in the ironworks along the north edge of the zone. There, numerous finds of iron scoria and rusted, deteriorated objects and discards were found in combination with a coin of Antony and Lepidus dated ca. 42 BCE and a *terra sigillata* fragment of a plate with the stamp ANTERO AVIL . . . (i.e., Anteros, slave of Avillius; ca. 10 BCE or later).[5] Also of economic significance is the increase in domestic fowl on the site, as testified in Well #1 by the sharp increase in the number of bones of chicken, goose, and swan from the time Cetamura became Roman. The presence of two types of chicken, including also chicks, indicates a well-developed practice of raising and consuming poultry on the

6.4. Silver denarius of Octavian. 30–27 BCE. Obv. bust of Victory.

6.5. Silver denarius of the fleet of Mark Antony. 32–31 BCE. Obv. Roman warship.

property.[6] No doubt one of the attractive aspects of the holding was the vineyards that had been developed in the fields around the hill and that evidently continued to flourish until Late Roman antiquity.

The Early Roman Empire

Well #1 also provides information about Cetamura during the early Roman Empire. In Well Group VI (ca. 30 BCE to 37 CE) appeared a number of coins of the Julio-Claudian period, including one type from the reign of Tiberius (14–37 CE), with obverse head of Augustus with radiant crown and the inscription DIVVS AVGVSTVS ("Divine Augustus"), and reverse altar with inscription PROVIDENT(IA) ("Providence").[7] There were two red-gloss stamps in locus 93, and one from locus 92 with the letters MMI, from the shop of Memmius of Arezzo, datable between 20 BCE and 10 CE.[8] The loci contained box flue tiles (*tubuli*) from the Roman baths, some cast lead cockle shells (probably feet of Roman situlae, as discussed below), a fragment of a Roman lamp, and two additional examples of a bone hairpin/stylus. Most notable is a bronze figurine of a calf or bull from locus 93 (fig. 6.6),[9] in a vigorous pose of jumping or perhaps kneeling. The right front foreleg is bent sharply backward and rests upon an extra supporting post (which also resembles a leg except that it is considerably thicker than the other legs of the creature). The piece can be confidently interpreted as votive and, along with polished pebbles and four miniature vessels in these loci, shows continuity in the sacred character of the well during Roman times. The numerous coins from the Roman Imperial loci likewise may be explained as ritual deposits. Numbers of astragali and tokens are dramatically reduced from this point on.

Well Group VII contained numerous coins, with none more important than the latest datable object in the group, a dupondius of Nero with obverse head of Nero and reverse SECVRITAS AVGVS(TA) ("Augustan Security") found in locus 91 (ca. 63 CE).[10] Also of interest from the same locus but obviously not useful for dating was a silver quinarius of Marcus Porcius Cato, with obverse head of Liber with ivy crown and reverse Victory seated (89 BCE).[11] No other Republi-

6.6. Bronze votive bull from Well #1.

can coins were found in this group of loci. All other coins were of bronze (the total for these loci was 48), featuring images of numerous members of the Julio-Claudian family: Augustus, Agrippa, Drusus, Antonia, Germanicus, Caligula, and Claudius; the reverses provide a variety of imperial messages. It is tempting to consider these as offerings honoring a cult of the imperial family, showing that the waters were still considered sacred though the divinities were new to the site.

Red-gloss stamps were sufficiently consistent with the numismatic evidence.[12] The datable stamps included in loci 90 and 88 were of L.IEGID, 20–10 BCE; in 88, of C.MVRI, with a stamp *in planta pedis* (the name is inserted into a footprint), i.e., after ca. 15/20 CE, when these stamps first appeared, and there were two more *in planta pedis* stamps (illegible) in 88 and 83 respectively. Roman lamps,[13] amphoras,[14] and glass[15] and great quantities of tile and brick from the baths also confirmed the dating.

Again the amount of material was enormous, but given that these loci are firmly established as Roman, less space is devoted to them here than to the Etruscan strata. Nonetheless, of the greatest significance is the series of Roman bronze vessels, eleven in all, found distributed in loci 91, 88, 86, 85, and 83. One is a pitcher (fig. 6.7), and all the rest are situlae, designated by letters from A to J.[16] These were uncovered in varying states of preservation and show variations in form and size, though so far, all are consistent with a date in the first century CE, as evident in many comparanda from Pompeii.[17] Situla F from locus 89 is well preserved and can give some idea of these buckets (fig. 6.8; F is on the right). At a height of 23 cm, it features a simple ovoid body tapering down to a base that is slightly bowed up, i.e., concave (diam. 17 cm). The rim (diam. 22 cm) is lightly flaring. Portions of the rim are missing, but it seems likely that the handles were never attached directly to it. Rather, an iron collar beneath the rim seems to have served to attach a handle and/or a chain.

Unearthed in Loci 89 and 88 were several lead situla feet, most shell form in design, detached from the Roman bronze vessels.[18] Among the significant artifacts found in association with the vessels were the following: a silver spoon;[19] a worked bone hinge in two joining parts;[20] a bone needle; two joining fragments of a bone stylus/hairpin;[21] a fragment of a painted terracotta plaque;[22] 12 votive vessels, many fragmentary; ceramic weights; Roman amphora fragments; Roman lamp fragments; and fragments of Roman blown-glass vessels.

Pollen analysis of Well Group VII shows a significant change in the landscape,[23] with a dramatic increase in evergreen holly oak (*Quercus ilex*), not unknown in Etruscan times but now competing strongly with the long-established deciduous oaks. The cause of the change in the forest could be due to the climate becoming drier, or to human intervention, or both. A curious find in locus 90 was a surprising amount of pollen of *Crocus etruscum*, a much higher percentage than could have occurred naturally, leading to the inference that someone intentionally dropped crocus flowers in the well. A similar phenomenon, not quite as pronounced, also appears in Etruscan loci.[24]

The Later Roman Empire

In the shaft of the well above all this, a dramatic change in the deposits was detectable, and this material constitutes Well Group VIII. Everything below this dividing point belonged to the centuries of actual

6.7. Bronze pitcher from Well #1.

6.8. Situlas J, H, and F from Well #1.

usage of the well, but above it there were many meters of debris typical of dumping, with a great amount of brick, tile, and stone. There was a huge volume and variety of materials that could be directly attributed to the dismantling of the Roman baths that once stood on Zone I not far from the well: burnt tile fragments and one brick probably from the bath furnace; paver bricks; box flue tile fragments; glass from window panes; a large segment of *cocciopesto*, the characteristic plaster and ceramic paving used in Roman baths; and fragments of plaster or stucco. Unearthed as well were segments of worked microbreccia stone that, when joined, formed a square, perforated slab, 35 by 36 cm (fig. 6.9), conjectured to be part of a drain.[25]

Late Antique ceramics and a few coins belonged to the lower strata of these dumps, but the practice of dumping went on literally for centuries. In the upper reaches of the shaft were discovered huge sandstone slabs that had been used for the covering of the well. These had originally been placed in a kind of corbelled arrangement with the slabs leaning against each other to produce a gabled effect (fig. 6.10). At the time of the discovery of the well by Tracchi some slabs were still *in situ*, but they collapsed into the shaft at a later moment, probably in the 1990s.[26]

Tracchi's colleague Fernando Bartolozzi extracted two segments of a sandstone wellhead in 1970;[27] amazingly, a third segment, constituting fully one-half of the head, was found forty-six years later in 2016 in a ground trench next to the well. All three parts fit together, indicating that they were once a monolithic feature, perforated with a round opening ca. 50 cm in diameter (fig. 6.11). The upper edges of the perforation are worn smooth, presumably by the constant usage of ropes to lower and pull back up the vessels that were securing water. Several fragments of what was probably the capstone were found, reconstructed as a stone ca. 50 cm in diameter, with a u-shaped iron handle inserted into drilled holes and secured by a lead filling (fig. 6.12).[28] All but one part of the capstone and handle were found in the Roman levels, suggesting that that is when the feature went out of use. It is unclear from the stratigraphy whether it, and the wellhead itself, had already been in use by the Etruscans, but there do exist comparisons for the type of opening from Etruscan Marzabotto and Vetulonia.[29]

6.9. Perforated granite slab, possibly from Roman baths, from Well #1.

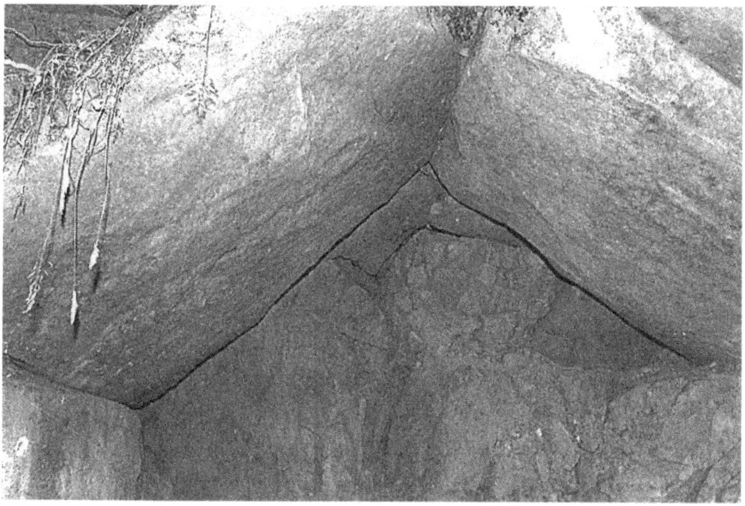

6.10. Stone vault formerly covering Well #1.

6.11. Wellhead from Well #1.

Sporadic evidence suggests that there was a human presence on the site of Cetamura in the middle years of the Roman Empire (e.g., coins of Trajan and Marcus Aurelius,[30] and African *sigillata* ceramics, associated with the second century CE), but thus far no building has been identified that can be tied to this chronology. Well #2 has revealed the principal evidence that there was a later occupation of the site, probably in the third and fourth centuries CE, when, as noted earlier, the structure was cleaned out and reused. So far, no particular area of Cetamura has been identified as the habitation associated with this period. A quite significant amount of pottery, particularly pitchers (fig. 6.13) and other vessels used for securing water, has been found, some of it featuring the incised wavy lines that are typical of late imperial and early medieval wares.[31] Of particular importance was the retrieval through flotation of more than four thousand grape pips that seem to belong to the period of the Late Roman Empire.

6.12. Well cap from Well #1.

6.13. Late Antique pitcher from Well #2.

7
Cetamura as a Community

The methodology for studying an Etruscan site as a community includes some of the same research questions as those used for a city. For both categories we make inquiries regarding the origin and development of the habitation, and how large the population was at its acme. Were there fortifications, and if so, of what type? What evidence is there for roads leading in and out of the settlements, and what kinds of connections do they establish? How was water provided? What kind of installations show religious activities, what kind of rituals are evident, and who are the gods? What kind of inscriptions occur? Was there extensive production? Can we say anything about how the site was governed or regulated? What was the nature of the cemeteries?

On the other hand, there are of course different kinds of questions to ask when the environment is not urban. How did small rural communities organize space? What kind of society was present? Was there in fact any kind of spectrum of society? To which major Etruscan cities was the site attached and how? Why was the community never larger or more heavily populated?

Most of these matters have been addressed earlier in this volume, but it remains to draw the information together and write the conclusions to the investigation.

The hill of Cetamura, though higher than many an Etruscan city,[1] provided a relatively limited space for settlement. Again and again the geophysical model for the cities of the Twelve Peoples is a large, relatively low, flat plateau, often volcanic, with abundant room for urban expansion. The sandstone hill of Cetamura is habitable only on the relatively flat Zones I (ca. 50 × 35 m) and II (ca. 70 × 60 m), as demonstrated by excavations, and according to Tracchi on two lower zones (see map 2), one of which is a corridor for communication and the other of which is smaller than Zone II. There is no room to expand on this type of mountainous terrain, which is so typical of the region of the Monti del Chianti. The population accommodated could not have been very large, probably no more than five hundred inhabitants at any given time, as opposed to the tens of thousands estimated for some Etruscan cities.[2] Presumably in the same pattern as most Etruscan sites, burials would not be made in the area of the living but rather on the slopes or on adjacent hills. Due to limited exploration in the area of Cetamura the cemeteries are not yet identified.

So far there is little to indicate that Etruscan Cetamura was a heavily fortified site. The most likely stronghold would have been on Zone I, but there is as yet no evidence of Etruscan defenses along the perimeter, since the zone was heavily reworked as part of the medieval *castrum*; and if anything was still preserved at that time it might have been torn down subsequently by the Florentines in 1198. On the north side, however, on the ridge between Zones I and II, there are hints of fortification: walls parallel to one another, seemingly as part of a gateway (see fig. 3.6). The ritual crevice of the late fourth century BCE stretched across the area that may have been the threshold of this gate (see fig. 2.2), and on top of the filled crevice was preserved a tract of kiln-fired bricks (see fig. 3.7). It is a fair hypothesis that such bricks were part of the gate system and thus the fortifications of the fourth century BCE.

On Zone II, all known perimeter walls seem to be parts of buildings rather than separate fortifications. Often these walls are of the same thickness as other walls within the same building. The masonry used is always the unmortared irregular style; there is no rectangular ashlar masonry or isodomic courses, which are often found in the great Etruscan cities such as Veii, Caere, Tarquinia, and others.[3] Given these reservations, it is perhaps better to be cautious about using such typological terminology for Cetamura as *fortezza d'altura* ("fortress on the heights"), *castellum* ("fortress or garrison"), or *oppidum* ("fortified hilltown").[4] H. Becker made a useful survey of sixteen small hilltop settlements of northern Etruria in the Hellenistic period that perhaps could be seen as fortified satellites of Fiesole or Volterra. She rightly acknowledged that Cetamura did not have evidence of Etruscan fortifications, but she argued nevertheless that its steepness meant that it fit the pattern she was attempting to identify.[5]

There may have been a spring at the base of the hill of Cetamura in antiquity, as suggested by the terrain, which seems to show the origin of a torrent at about 200 meters below the northernmost walls. Certainly the site exhibits the traditional Etruscan concern for water supply, with two deep wells so far discovered, and a system of drainage and catchment in Structures A, B, and D in the Artisans' Quarter, though it is perhaps a little surprising that more installations have not appeared, given how ubiquitous Etruscan provisions for water management are in both cities and cemeteries.[6]

Access to the site was probably, exactly as today, on the steep north side of the hill. Tracchi's clearing on "Zone D" (see map 2) suggests access to the site on the southwest as well, but the mural installations are quite uninvestigated for dating. In any case it seems unlikely that there are any other entrances to the site beside these two. Both could have connected rather easily with the road system hypothesized by Tracchi as running along the ridges of the Chianti Mountains and connecting sites at Radda (Poggio La Croce) and Castellina in Chianti (Montecalvario, Salivolpe, Fonterutoli) and farther away at Volterra (ca. 60 km), Fiesole (ca. 60 km), Arezzo (ca. 50 km), Siena (ca. 35 km), and Chiusi (ca. 85 km). So far, the evidence for networking with these cities and settlements is rather limited, but may show connections in architecture, metalworking, and pottery. The masonry of buildings of the Late Etruscan periods at Cetamura evokes comparisons with buildings of Fiesole, but the similarities may be superficial, having more to do with the fact that both sites exploited a fairly dense and durable gray sandstone. The ironworks on Zone II will have received ores from the Etruscan coast, probably Populonia, a connection that seems confirmed by the finding of situla L, with its strong associations with Populonia. Certainly it is no surprise to see ceramics painted in red or black that were imported from Volterra and Arezzo.

As for agriculture as practiced by the Etruscan inhabitants of Cetamura, a great quantity of data has been collected and with further study may reveal a detailed chronological picture. It is generally agreed that the site itself was too high for cultivation of crops, but it is clear that over a long period of time there were well-established vineyards in the surrounding areas, lower in altitude and perfectly well suited for the growing of grapes. The presence of grains is certainly attested, as in the offerings of Votive Feature 1 in the second century BCE, where there was evidence of barley, emmer wheat, and common bread wheat. The same deposit gave evidence of fruits such as apple, sorb apple, and pear, and the two wells indicated the presence of walnut, pine nut, cherries, plums, olive, and hazelnut. The quantification of these items (and the laboratory analysis of all pollen and other organic remains) may yet tell more about the chronological sequence of exploitation and the relative priority of the various crops.

It is not possible to speak of an origin and development of habitation at Cetamura. Instead there seem to have been periodic occupations, beginning probably with a small Archaic settlement on Zone I, linked only loosely with the princely inhabitants of Castellina in Chianti or the area of Castelnuovo Berardenga in the late seventh and sixth centuries BCE. This settlement disappeared by the fifth century BCE, and was followed around the middle of the fourth century or later by the arrival of a substantial, well-connected group, probably utilizing mainly Zone I. A true explosion of activity came around 300 BCE, when great earth-moving works were undertaken on Zone II, allowing for the building of the deep walls of Structures B and C, as well as Structures H, K, and part of D, and also the two wells. A vigorous population was required to accomplish all of this. There is no clear break before the next spree of building around 150 or 125 BCE; this period may represent mainly new waves of settlers joining the established group. They built Structure A and Building L, and reworked and reused B and probably other existing structures.

What was the source of prosperity for the inhabitants of Cetamura during these periods? When investigating the nature of the economy and society at Cetamura during these last three Etruscan stages, it is necessary to talk about several other factors. How did the Etruscans of the Middle and Late periods organize space? Perhaps most intriguing is the discovery that there was a designated artisans' zone, a pattern that had appeared already in the Archaic period at Poggio Civitate di Murlo, where an astonishing open shed-like building 52 meters long accommodated a number of crafts.[7] The buildings dedicated to craftsmanship at Cetamura were arranged instead in a cluster of separate rectangular structures (A, B, C, D, J, K, H, N), probably having walls as well as roofs. Rather extensive paving provided for work areas that could easily be kept clean. The close relationship of these structures is emphasized by the fact that they are all oriented on the same north–south axis.

Certainly the actual production of various kinds of goods was essential for the community. Probably the location of the quarters on the edge of the site on a lower zone is at least partly related to a desire to control pollution and noise. But the overall importance of industry for the community of ancient Cetamura is indicated by its location next to one of the two entranceways to the site. There the artisans could receive immediate attention for their production of textiles, iron objects, brick, tile and loom weights, and modest objects of adornment such as earrings, polished stones, and possibly carved gems.

What was the nature of this stratum of society? Most likely some of the artisans—the weavers and spinners—were female, while the workers in iron and ceramics were most likely male. It cannot be ruled out that children were in the workforce. It is frequently assumed that Etruscan society was basically made up of nobles and their servants or slaves.[8] This model is exemplified by imported objects at Cetamura such as the third-century Greco-Italic amphora from the Latin firm of M. Lurius, which features the stamp of the Greek artisan signed as EUTACHEI (discussed in chapter 3). The small bronze measuring tool dating to the first century BCE (see fig. 5.16) with the stamp of PHILEM, not likely to have been made at Cetamura, provides another example. The various stamps on Arretine pottery from Cetamura include Greek, Latin, and Etruscan names of owners and artists, in a picture that is far from clear but in any case is not relevant for the period of the workshops at Cetamura.[9] Further, none of the examples cited above is purely an Etruscan case, nor is there any evidence that these items were actually made at Cetamura.

It seems likely that the oft-invoked dichotomy of Etruscan elites versus nonelites is not meaningful here. There is absolutely no evidence so far of Cetamura being the possession of some local noble who would profit from the production on the site. The artisans who are so much in evidence at Cetamura may have formed a class of their own, as individuals who worked with their hands but who also managed money, and at least some of whom were probably literate. We recall that the part of the site that has yielded the most coins (apart from the wells) and most of the Etruscan inscriptions is precisely this complex.

Also significant is the close, even symbiotic, relationship between the artisans' zone and the sanctuary, for which the workers probably provided offerings for visitors and made offerings themselves. A sanctuary may have already been present in the third century BCE or earlier, but what has survived is almost entirely of the second half of the second century BCE. The difference in orientation of Building L and the structures of the artisans' zone may be due to this chronological factor or, more likely, ritual considerations that respected the southeast area of the skies and of the site itself.

We must also inquire as to who were the actual sponsors of the sanctuary of Late Etruscan Phase II. A key piece of evidence is Votive Feature 1, probably a foundation deposit, in which the several layers of material and the numerous objects (totaling ca. 50) suggest a lengthy ritual and participation by a group. The objects found were not "elite," but the act of offering suggests commitment to a body of valued material. The pottery was local or regional, almost all without color coat, but of a remarkable variety that indicates careful selection. The metals included numerous pieces of iron, especially nails of many different types. A reasonable working hypothesis is that the group that made the offerings included artisans from the community, since the objects are quite consistent with such a segment of the society. Thus these individuals may have played a role of some authority in religious (and political?) decisions about the settlement.

As for the gods who were worshiped in the sanctuary, it is interesting that so far there is no trace of the principal deities of the Etruscans, such as Tinia or Uni. They appear in the cults of great cities such as Caere, Tarquinia, and Cortona, and elsewhere[10]; indeed for Arezzo the most famous Etruscan dedication, the Chimera, seems to have been a gift to Tin(ia).[11] The extensive potters' quarter at Veii seems to be situated near a great temple, possibly to Uni (known as Juno to the invading Romans).[12] The recent spectacular discovery of a great stone stele at Poggio Colla (Vicchio) in the Mugello with the names of Tin(ia) and Uni adds considerable interest to the spectrum of these deities.[13] Poggio Colla, a fortified hilltop sanctuary with artisanal activity, is similar to Cetamura, but the offerings there are, on the whole, of a greater monetary value. Also, the site preserves remnants of what must have been a monumental stone temple. So in a way, this example reinforces the generalization emerging in this discussion that Tinia and Uni are gods of larger political and social entities.

The inscriptions of Cetamura refer instead to Leinth, otherwise unknown as a deity of cult, and Lur, whose name is known widely but rarely at a major city.[14] It is interesting, however, to note that on more than one occasion the worship of Lur seems to be linked with the cult of Tinia. A foot of a bronze cup inscribed with the name of Lur was discovered in a sacred area at Bolsena where two altars to Tinia were found. His name occurs next to the name of Tinia on the well-known lead tablet from Magliano. And on a mirror of the style of Vulci, Lur appears as a prophetic figure reciting under inspiration from Tinia (fig. 7.1).

Looking at ritual behaviors at Cetamura, and the presence of divining devices such as astragali, tokens, and wooden tablets, it seems appropriate to interpret the gods of Cetamura as having to do with fortune, fate, and good luck. The still mysterious inscriptions with the

7.1. Engraved Etruscan bronze mirror with scene of Lur (*left*) and Tinia (*center*). Ca. 350 BCE. Moscow, Pushkin Museum of Fine Arts (drawing by K. Mortimore).

ligature *ALP* also may refer to an abstract quality, identified in the Etruscan word *alpan,* meaning "good will" or "with good will." Only two inscriptions tell us the names of worshipers, Cluntni and Lausini, single names that need not be noble. In sum, Lur and Leinth are gods that may have had personal or artisanal connections, but were not necessarily related to wealthy and powerful members of Etruscan society, nor did they play a role in organized government. Further, there is no evidence that their cult related to healing, since the terracotta anatomical votives so common in Etruria are absent so far from Cetamura.

All in all, Cetamura presents a vivid contrast with the grand Etruscan cities and other smaller communities as well. The discovery of a sanctuary closely related to a well-developed artisans' quarter in a relatively isolated rural context presents a window on the practice of Etruscan religion within a society that is neither elite nor nonelite, but seems to hold a particular social context associated with the life of artisans.

8
Cetamura after Antiquity

After more than six centuries of almost continuous habitation by Etruscans and Romans, Cetamura appears to have been abandoned for a while. Documents of the Middle Ages, however, make it clear that the land came to be valued again, for a succession of owners is recorded in the eleventh and twelfth centuries CE, including the Badia a Coltibuono, to whom the property belongs today.[1] One document, dated to ca. 1172, refers to the site as a *castrum*, a term that normally means "castle,"[2] and raises injunctions against the inhabitants of the place, evidently members of the powerful Chianti family of the Firidolfi (Ricasoli), because they had been abusing the monks of Coltibuono. Several documents also call the place Civitamura, "Wall City," reflecting the conspicuous features of the site. Especially on Zone I there is evidence of medieval construction, including a substantial fortification wall at the north edge.[3] The site was seemingly attacked by the Florentines in 1198, who may have razed the existing castle to the ground to subdue the Firidolfi. In any case, there is little left of the *castrum* but the in-ground foundations, some of which are actually quite imposing (fig. 8.1).

The remains of anything Etruscan on Zone I were mostly obliterated and the Roman baths were probably completely dismantled by this time, with usable building materials carried away. Fragmentary tile and brick were dumped into Well #1. A massive dumping episode in Well #2—of numerous and sometimes huge stones of the type used in Late Etruscan Phase II as well as some Roman worked pieces of travertine—suggests that a similar situation obtained on Zone II.

8.1. Foundation walls of the medieval *castrum* on Zone I.

There are scraps of evidence, chiefly Archaic Sienese majolica, that the high defensible site experienced traffic during the fifteenth and sixteenth centuries, probably during wars between Siena and Florence.[4] Then, an earthquake rocked the zone of Chianti in 1558. After that all fell silent at Cetamura.

Because there is no modern construction present on the hill, exploration and excavation have been facilitated. The site was rediscovered as noted earlier in 1964 by Alvaro Tracchi of San Giovanni Valdarno, who was researching Etruscan and Roman road systems and made a survey of two hundred sites of the Chianti and Valdarno region.[5] He felt that Cetamura del Chianti was his most important discovery, as a well-developed regional center of Etruscan and Roman times. Without actually excavating, he was able to identify and map numerous walls on four different zones of the site (see map 2). His discoveries were duly reported to the superintendent for archaeological resources in Tuscany at that time, Guglielmo Maetzke, in Florence. Thus it was when J. J. Reich, a professor at the Florida State University Study Center in Florence, inquired in 1972 of the superintendency about the possibility of securing a permit for FSU faculty and students to excavate an archaeological site in Tuscany, Cetamura was suggested.[6] Graduate student Clark Sykes organized the project and served as field director in the early campaigns. Excavations have taken place almost annually since 1973. Patrick Rowe, as overall site supervisor after Sykes, played a key role in producing the first surveyed maps. The grid that he established in 1978 has remained the basis of the mapping of the entire site up to the present time (see map 3).

Revelations about the site have been especially significant since the uncovering of Roman baths in 1984; of the Etruscan artisans' zone in 1994 and following; and of the religious sanctuary of the Etruscans in 2006 and following. Through these years and successively there were some thirteen campaigns to excavate Well #1, culminating in five seasons of work and completion of the project by the firm Ichnos: Archeologia, Ambiente e Sperimentazione (president, Francesco Cini) of Montelupo Fiorentino, in collaboration with Cheryl L. Sowder of Jacksonville University.[7] The results were highly important for linking together the various discoveries to create a continuous narrative about the history of the site as presented in this volume. Finally, work in Well #2 on Zone II was completed by the same team in 2016; while this Etruscan well actually lacked clear documentation for the Etruscan period, it revealed surprising evidence that Cetamura was occupied as late as the third and fourth centuries CE and provided some indications regarding what may have happened to Etruscan buildings on Zone II. The discovery of a Roman coin repository in 2015–2016 was crucial for understanding the key moment of transition from Etruscan to Roman occupation of the site.

Professors and students from several other American universities have played key roles in excavating, processing, and studying the mass of information that has been emerging from all of these projects. Lora Holland of the University of North Carolina–Asheville has directed the laboratory, ushering through many thousands of finds, while Laurel Taylor, also of UNC-A, has served in collaboration with Charles Ewell, of the University of Syracuse and New York University in Florence, to plan and direct much of the actual fieldwork in the trenches, bringing their own students to contribute to the success of the project. Publications on Cetamura by these members of the team and studies by many other scholars and students are listed in the bibliography of this volume. As acknowledged in the preface, the conservation and restoration carried out by Studio Arts College International (SACI), under the supervision of Renzo Giachetti, Roberta Lapucci, and Nòra Marosi over a period of more than twenty years, beginning in 1997, has been of the utmost importance, not only for the urgent and proper care of the artifacts but also because of the stimulus provided for the didactic aspects and research projects.[8]

The history of Cetamura emerging from the site itself should be viewed against the backdrop of the Chianti landscape and environment, now under intensive study and interpretation on the basis of organic remains from the two wells. Fittingly, the main outlines have been obtained by a team of prominent Italian scientists, including Gianna Giachi, Marta Mariotti Lippi, Miria Mori Secci, Elisabetta Castiglioni, Michela Cottini, and Mauro Rottoli.[9] They have revealed that the landscape of Cetamura today is not so very different from that of Roman times, with a predominantly hardwood forest, although chestnut is more conspicuous now, and that the principal difference from Etruscan times was the proliferation of holly oak that occurred in the Roman period. The animal population, as shown by Ornella Fonzo and Chiara Corbino, included boar and deer (as may be seen in the woods of Cetamura today) but farm and pasturing animals—pig (especially), sheep/goat, and cow—were extremely important for the economy from Etruscan times; the raising of poultry was central to the Roman period.[10]

No discoveries have been more important than the revelations about vineyards in the ancient Chianti region. It is clear from the study of grape pips from as early as the fourth century BCE that the Etruscans recognized the great potential of the region for growing grapes for wine and that their practices were appreciated and continued by the Roman owners of Cetamura. Thanks to recent studies by scientists Nathan Wales and Laurent Bouby[11] of the DNA content of several samples and of forms of hundreds of waterlogged seeds from the two wells, it is possible to observe that there was a great tradition and continuity in making a Chianti wine with white (probably) berries over a period of some six hundred years.

A recent study of the grape seeds from Well #1,[12] undertaken independently from the Cetamura research team, unfortunately suffers from numerous errors of fact and methodology due to a lack of knowledge of the site and of Etruscan culture and civilization. The authors argue that around 200 BCE at Cetamura there was an increase in grape pip size, reflecting the introduction of the pruning knife under influences from Romans and Phoenicians. The response to the article[13] makes it clear that the authors did not realize that no Cetamura pips have been dated to the period 200–150 BCE and thus no data are available to support an increase in pip size around 200 BCE. Further, the pruning knife was known to the Etruscans from as early as the Iron Age (seventh–sixth centuries BCE) and hardly would have been introduced in Tuscany for the first time around 200 BCE.

Knowledge of Etruscan viticulture is expanding greatly, and there is an increasing opportunity to formulate a history of its development in pre-Imperial Italy.[14] The grape pips from Cetamura, numbering more than forty-five hundred and representing a stretch of time of roughly six hundred years, show promise of adding to the narrative. Research is still in progress and may yet reveal a great deal more about the Etruscan and Roman forerunners of the Chianti wines of modern times.

APPENDIX

A Timeline of History for Cetamura del Chianti

Ca. 20,000–10,000 years before the present—Upper Paleolithic period; presence of hunters in Tuscany, possibly at Cetamura; flint tools from Zone II

Seventh–sixth centuries BCE—Etruscan Archaic period; indication of timber building on Zone I; bucchero pottery

Fifth century BCE—No evidence of habitation at Cetamura

359–351 BCE—"Etruscan Wars" between Rome and Etruscan cities of southern Etruria (Tarquinia and Caere)

Ca. 350/325 BCE—Repopulation of the site; crevice deposit between Zones I and II. Gateway to Zone I on the north side.

302 BCE—Civil unrest at Arretium (Arezzo) against the noble Cilnii, with Roman intervention

280, 273, 264 BCE—Romans conquer Vulci, Caere, Volsinii (Orvieto)

Ca. 300–150 BCE—Late Etruscan ("Hellenistic") period, Phase I at Cetamura. Structures B, C, K, H, M, N. Artisans' Quarter on Zone II. Wine grapes cultivated.

217 BCE—Time of Second Punic War. March of Hannibal from Faesulae to Arretium

205 BCE—Time of Second Punic War. Fleet of Scipio Africanus equipped by Etruscan cities, including Arretium

Second century BCE—Building of Via Cassia, highway through northern Etruria

Ca. 150–100/75 BCE—Late Etruscan ("Hellenistic") period, Phase II. Structures A, B (phase II), D, L.

91–88 BCE—Social Wars of Romans with Italian allied peoples

87–80 BCE—Civil War between Marius and Sulla

82–80 BCE—Siege of Volterra by Sulla; destruction of Faesulae and subsequent colonization by Sulla's veterans

63 BCE—Conspiracy of Catiline with base at Faesulae

Ca. 28 BCE—Cetamura hypothesized to become the holding of a Roman veteran

Ca. 27 BCE–14 CE—Rule of Augustus (Octavian). Roman habitation. Construction of baths on Zone I, Area G. Exploitation of vineyards. Raising of poultry.

First century CE—Julio-Claudian emperors. Continuation of Roman habitation.

Second century CE—Sporadic evidence of Roman presence.

Third–fourth centuries CE—Period of Roman soldier emperors. Cleaning and reuse of Well #2. Abundant pottery. Exploitation of vineyards.

Fifth–sixth centuries—No evidence of habitation at Cetamura.

Seventh–eighth centuries—Period of Langobard rule in Italy. Langobards in Tuscany. No evidence of habitation at Cetamura.

Ca. 800—Probable first construction of church of San Lorenzo at Badia a Coltibuono, by Ieremias of the Firidolfi of Monte Grossoli

1037—Founding of Badia a Coltibuono, sponsored by the Firidolfi

1051—Founding of a hospice at Badia a Coltibuono

1066—Land at Civitamura donated to Coltibuono by Petrus, son of Bonitius

1121—Land at Civitamura purchased by Actio and his brothers Iohanni and Petrus from Feralmo and Ugo, sons of Iohanni. The land had been worked by Teutio da Pian Dumule.

1124—Land at Civitamura donated by Actio to Coltibuono.

1135—Sale of some land at Civitamura to Coltibuono by Petrus, son of Actio

1170s—Civitamura referred to as *castrum*, probably owned by the Firidolfi family

1198—Probable date of the destruction of the *castrum* at Cetamura by the Florentines

1452, 1478—Invasion of Chianti by the Aragonese

1554—Conquest of Siena (and Chianti) by the Medici of Florence

1558—Earthquake in Chianti

NOTES

CHAPTER 1. INTRODUCTION

1. I thank cartographer Kurtis Butler for these coordinates. Cf. the relevant 1:50,000 Carta archeologica della provincia di Siena (fol. 113.II in Valenti 1995), which is based on cartography of the Istituto Geografico Militare of Italy.

2. Tracchi 1966, 1971, 1978. The following, though outdated, are among the essential earlier scholarly references: Mangani 1986; *Atlante Toscana*, 206 (no. 73); Valenti 1995:253 (no. 182). See also note 4 below.

3. Reich 1972, 1973, 1980. De Grummond 1985, 1991, 2000.

4. Pagliai 2008:32 (doc. 61, 1066), 141 (doc. 309, 1121), 146 (doc. 319, 1124), 163 (doc. 361, 1135).

5. Boglione 1993:47 (document from the Archivio di Stato di Firenze, ca. 1172).

6. There is another site called Cetamura near Castelnuovo Berardenga, also in the territory of Siena. Cetamura della Berardenga, like Cetamura del Chianti, is known for Etruscan, Roman, and medieval remains, but unlike the Chianti site, it has not been formally excavated. See Tracchi 1978:36 (no. 33); *Atlante Toscana*, 246 (no. 203); Valenti 1995:329 (no. 120). It too was called Civita Mura in the Middle Ages, but there can be no doubt that the Civitamura mentioned in the documents cited above, notes 4–5, is the Chianti site.

7. De Grummond, Giachetti, and Marosi 2009. See notes 2–3 for other basic bibliography. Bizzarri and Soren (2016:136) incorporate Cetamura into a survey of Etruscan sites important for revealing domestic architecture.

8. De Grummond 2017.

9. Bouby, Ivorra, and Terral 2017; Wales, Ramos-Madrigal, and Gilbert 2017.

10. Cottini 2009; Mori Secci 2009; Wilkens 2009; Castiglioni, Cottini, and Rottoli 2017; Giacchi 2017; Mariotti Lippi and Mori Secci 2017; Corbino and Fonzo 2017.

CHAPTER 2. EARLY AND MIDDLE ETRUSCAN PERIODS

1. Layton 2009.

2. Pianu 2000. Rasmussen 1979:2–3 discusses standards and variants in bucchero. Layton 2009:27 details the wide variation in the fabric of Cetamura bucchero.

3. Milani 1905; Pernier 1916; Firmati 2014:78–81 (entry by G. C. Cianferoni). On early discoveries at Castellina, sometimes connected with the tumulus of Montecalvario, see de Grummond 2018a.

4. Layton 2009:23–26 for a survey of bucchero found in Chianti.

5. Layton 2009:34; Valenti 1995:271, pl. 107.19 (entry by I. Alfani and F. Bracciali).

6. Layton 2009:32; Mangani 1988–1989:69, fig. 59.174. In general on Castelnuovo Berardenga: Mangani 1985.

7. Layton 2009:40–42, 47–48, and Bocci 1965:169, fig. 29.1763, and 190, pl. 55.3005.

8. De Grummond, Giachetti, and Marosi 2009:129–134.

9. Wilkens 2009.

10. Cianferoni 1984:67. Valenti 1995:273–274, pl. 108.31 (entry by M. Zannoni). De Grummond 2000:23 (cat. no. 6), placed in the group from Volterra called "Ferrara Group T 585," dated ca. 325–300 BCE.

11. Cf. a two-handled *kylix* (drinking cup) found at Castelnuovo Berardenga, locality Bosco Le Pici, Tomb F, dating to the middle of the fourth century BCE: Goggioli 2012:138. On Atticizing pottery in Italy, see Hayes 1984:43 and following.

12. De Grummond, Giachetti, and Marosi 2009:132–133 and pl. 27.155. For Grotti, Monteroni d'Arbia, see Cristofani 1979:70–82 (entries by E. Mangani and L. Cimino); Cianferoni 2001:86–87; and *Atlante Toscana*, 306, no. 78.

13. For bibliography see notes 31–35 of chapter 3.

14. Robertson 1989; De Grummond, Bare, and Meilleur 2000; De Grummond 2000:31–36; De Grummond, Giachetti, and Marosi 2009:159–164; Bagnasco Gianni 2014a; De Grummond 2017:103–105; Bagnasco Gianni and de Grummond forthcoming.

15. Bagnasco Gianni 2014a:208–209.

16. Hargis 2007; De Grummond, Giachetti, and Marosi 2009:131–132 (cat. no. 153).

17. See de Grummond 2017:86–87 (nos. 32–33), 98–100 (nos. 54–55, 57–58), 178–179 (no. 171).

18. On Monteroni d'Arbia, see note 12 above; Pasqui 1997; and Pericci 2018: 69–70 (no. 20.1). On San Martino: Cianferoni 2001. On Bosco Le Pici: Goggioli 2012.

CHAPTER 3. LATE ETRUSCAN PHASE I

1. Recounted well in regard to material culture in Etruria in general by Haynes (2000:306 and 327–330). Longer studies, with rich bibliographies, are Jolivet 2014 and Ceccarelli 2016.

2. Livy 10.3.2; 10.5.13. Camporeale 2009:72–74. Harris 1971:61–64.

3. On the concept of Hellenistic, especially as regards material culture, see for example Ling 1988 and Price 1988, making the usual connection with Greek influence in the creation and patronage of kingdoms of the eastern Mediterranean during the period from the death of Alexander (323 BCE) until the defeat of Antony and Cleopatra by Octavian (31 BCE). In fact Cetamura during this period shows almost no awareness of Hellenistic kingdoms, nor is there much to refer to Greek influence. For Chianti in the "Hellenistic" period, see Giroldini 2017:26–27.

4. De Grummond 2005.

5. De Grummond 2005:34.

6. De Grummond 2017. See especially Sowder 2017 and Cini, Cecchini, and Violetti 2017.

7. De Grummond 2017. See especially Sowder 2017 and Cini, Cecchini, and Violetti 2017.

8. Created in 2015 at the Florida State University Facility for Arts Research, under the supervision of Windham Graves, the FAR laboratory director.

9. Published extensively in de Grummond 1985; de Grummond 1991; de Grummond, Rowe, Marrinan et al. 1994; de Grummond, Rowe, Ewell et al. 1999; de Grummond 2000:17–29; de Grummond, Giachetti, and Marosi 2009; de Grummond 2017:182.

10. Bonfante (1986b:5–6) included Cetamura as a significant example of "nonfunerary archaeology" that may provide new information about town planning, hydraulics, and fortifications. To date it is not possible to confirm a street pattern at the site, which in itself may be an important and interesting feature of the settlement. The lack of a true fortification wall on Zone II is also unusual.

11. Ewell 2000 is fundamental. See also de Grummond 2001; de Grummond, Giachetti, and Marosi 2009:107–118; Davis and Kortum 2014; Ewell 2014.

12. Cottini 2009:187.

13. The kiln fits best with Cuomo di Caprio type IId, a square plan with central partition and two *praefurnia*: Cuomo di Caprio 1985:141.

14. Cottini 2009:187.

15. Davis and Kortum 2014.

16. See especially the discussion and the categories of ritual activity analyzed by M. Bonghi Jovino (2005:33–34); de Grummond (2011:73–77); and Ewell (2014: 223–232).

17. Olcese 2012:96–97 lists only potential kiln activity in the commune of Castelnuovo Berardenga: a *fornace* at Gaggiola is of Roman date; at I Caggi, the dating is of the second century BCE and the soil is described as reddened, but no structure is reported; at Monteaperti, the activity is dated from the first century BCE and later; at Pontiganello and San Polo the dating is of the fourth–fifth centuries CE. The entry on Cetamura, 97–98, is accurate in its description of Structure K, but the internal red-slip pottery from Cetamura taken from illustrations in Peña 1990 (pl. 1.XXIX) did not come from Structure K and has nothing to do with it. There is no evidence that pottery was ever fired in this kiln.

18. Curri and Sorbelli 1973 remains the basic study. A fuller survey of known Etruscan kilns is in Ewell 2000:54–80. Add Bon-Harper 2011, on the kiln workshop at Podere Funghi, near Poggio Colla; and Tuck 2009, on the third-century BCE kiln workshop at Vescovado di Murlo. The closest comparanda for the ground plan of Stucture K come from the site of Marcianello, Chiusi, especially kilns D (late third–early second century BCE, close in date to Cetamura Structure K), F (middle of second century BCE), and G (second half of second and beginning of first century BCE): published by Pucci and Mascione 2003.

19. See Hackworth 1993 on the various weaving utensils known before the excavation of Well #1 and their distribution, which is concentrated in the Artisans' Quarter.

20. Taylor 2015:134 and fig. 8.

21. De Grummond 2017:194 (cat. no. 190; entry by K. Linnamaa).

22. Pecci and Cau Ontiveros 2017. It was not possible, however, to confirm that the residues from wine and meat were deposited at the same moment. For a description of the ceramic paste, which is not a standard Cetamura fabric, see de Grummond 2017:194 (cat. no. 189).

23. De Grummond 2017:195–196 (cat. nos. 192 and 193; entries by K. Linnamaa). Comparanda for the bowl date it to the late third or early second century BCE.

24. De Grummond 2017:195 (cat. no. 191; entry by K. Linnamaa).

25. Taylor 2015:137–139, figs. 10–12.

26. Martelli 1981; Becker 2017. Concise treatment of the industrial zone of Poggio della Porcareccia at Populonia: Romualdi 1993:106–109.

27. Two characteristic black-gloss bowls with off-set rims date to the third or early second century BCE; de Grummond 2017:185–186 (cat. nos. 176–177; entries by de Grummond and C. Miller). C. Miller has prepared a full catalogue of pottery (unpublished) from inside Structure K, including numerous examples of local Cetamura wares and black-gloss ceramics, but no red-gloss, such as Volterran presigillata (see below), has been found. Pottery associated with ritual from inside Structure K is discussed above (with figs. 3.10–3.12).

28. Black-gloss pottery from Cetamura has been studied and published extensively. The unpublished MA thesis of M. Houston (1978)—on caches of black-gloss

from Structures A and B dating mainly from the second and first centuries BCE—remains fundamental. Curry (1996) dated pottery from the refuse area of Structure K to the third century BCE. Exhibition catalogs contain numerous examples: de Grummond 2000; de Grummond, Giachetti, and Marosi 2009; de Grummond 2017. Peña and Gallimore (2014:76) provide an excellent review of black-gloss pottery in northern Etruria and argue on the basis of clay samples for manufacture of some of the Cetamura black-gloss pottery at Arezzo, without rejecting the long-standing common hypothesis that some came from Volterra. Houston (1978:125–126) had already hypothesized both Volterra and Arezzo.

29. The most important study of this Etruscan ware is Cristofani and Cristofani-Martelli 1972. Williams 1996 was the first careful study of its presence at Cetamura. Key stamped examples of the bowls are published in de Grummond 2000:26 (cat. nos. 25–27; entries by J. L. Borek) and de Grummond 2017:128 (cat. no. 94) (here fig. 3.23).

30. Peña and Gallimore 2014:77 give a valuable description of the ware, under the rubric of North Etrurian Red-Slip Ware (NERSW). Unfortunately I find quite unlikely the dating proposed for the Cetamura samples in which the author(s) argue repeatedly that the "date can be pushed back to ca. 180 BCE" or earlier (137, 138, 139, 140). On the other hand the samples that are cited as having "manufacture commenced prior to ca. 150/125 BCE" are sufficiently consistent with all other indicators of the dating of the ware at Cetamura. Figure 3.23, for example, was found in strata of Well #1 dated to ca. 150–100 BCE (Well Group III) and 100–50 BCE (Well Group IV). No sherds of this red-gloss ware were found in the strata dated from ca. 300–150 BCE. For further discussion of the stratigraphy of Well #1, see chapter 5.

31. First studied by Sowder (1978 and 1984). The nomenclature for Cetamura fabrics was established by J. T. Peña in 1987–88, when he served as director of the Cetamura laboratory; see the "Introductory Note" in de Grummond 2000:22. Note also the important observations made about "common ware ceramics," in de Grummond 2017:132–137 (introduction by L. Banducci; cat. nos. 100–110; entries by Banducci).

32. Tracchi (1978:19) refers to this fabric as "impasto scuro con granuli bianchi." At Poggio La Croce, it was described as "fabric with white inclusions" (Cresci and Viviani 1995:153, note 3; see also Cresci et al. 1995:277–278).

33. Tracchi (1978:19) describes the fabric as "l'argilla granulosa arancione."

34. Tracchi (1978:19) refers to this fabric as "l'argilla granulosa chiara." Cresci and Viviani (1995:153, note 3) call it "light-colored grainy fabric." See also Cresci et al. 1995:278–279. It circulated widely in the territories of Faesulae (Fiesole) and Volterra: *Archeologia urbana a Fiesole*, 129–131, 199.

35. Tracchi (1978:24) refers to this fabric as "argilla figulina arancione."

36. De Grummond 2017:179 (cat. no. 172; entry by N. de Grummond and

K. Kaplan). Residual analysis of Dolium A, however, was inconclusive. Further, no evidence was found during excavation of dry foodstuffs such as grain.

37. Colonna and de Grummond 2007. Rix and Meiser 2014: Vt 3.10, Vt 3.11.

38. De Grummond 2011.

39. De Grummond 2000:35 (cat. no. 110).

40. De Grummond and Rix 1984. De Grummond 2000:35 (cat. no. 108). Rix and Meiser 2014: Vt 2.19.

41. De Grummond 2000:35 (cat. no. 107). Rix and Meiser 2014: Vt 2.2.

42. For bibliography on sigla at Cetamura, see note 14 of chapter 2.

43. Studied by Cha (2015). See also de Grummond 2017:138–143 (introduction by Cha and de Grummond; cat. nos. 111–118; entries by Cha).

44. See Bagnasco Gianni and de Grummond forthcoming, and the website of the International Etruscan Sigla Project, edited by G. Bagnasco Gianni and N. T. de Grummond: http://159.149.130.120/IESP/iesp_intro.php.

45. De Grummond, Giachetti, and Marosi 2009: 121 (cat. no. 13); de Grummond 2010; Hansson 2005:45, pl. 7.30.

46. Hansson 2005.

47. Poggio La Croce: Hansson 2005:47; de Grummond 2010: fig. 24. Now in the Museo Archeologico del Chianti, Castellina in Chianti. Castiglion Fiorentino: Hansson 2002 and 2005:45, pl. 7.30; de Grummond 2010: fig. 23.

48. De Grummond, Giachetti, and Marosi 2009:123–124 (cat. nos. 136, 138, and 139).

49. De Grummond, Giachetti, and Marosi 2009:124 (cat. nos. 141, 144, 145). See also the discussion in chapter 5 of this volume, in connection with tokens from Well #1.

50. Rolfo 2009.

51. De Grummond 2000: pl. 52b.

52. De Grummond 2017:199–202.

53. De Grummond 2017:71–77 (cat. nos. 9–17, 19; entries by E. Castiglioni, M. Cottini, G. Giachi, and M. Rottoli, with N. de Grummond). Discussed in more detail below in chapter 5.

54. Mariotti Lippi and Mori Secci 2017. On pollen samples taken from Lago di Accesa, an ironworking area, see Wiman 2014:18, where there is a description of the time, ca. 300 BCE, when forest was decreasing and there was a rising amount of wheat, olives, and wild grasses.

55. Corbino and Fonzo 2017.

56. Bouby, Ivorra, and Terral 2017.

57. Wales, Ramos-Madrigal, and Gilbert 2017.

58. See de Grummond 2018b and the discussion at the end of chapter 8 for some of the latest issues raised by the pips.

CHAPTER 4. LATE ETRUSCAN PHASE II

1. Cavallo (1992:9) reviews the various members of the gens Cassia who could have been sponsor(s) of the road. The exact date is not known and various scenarios have been argued. The possible dates are all in the second century: Harris (1971:167) favors 171 or 154 BCE, while others favor 125 BCE. C. Cassius Longinus, consul in 171 and censor in 154 BCE, is regarded as the most likely sponsor.

2. Structures A and B have been discussed extensively: de Grummond 1985; de Grummond et al. 1994:98–108; de Grummond 2000:17–18; de Grummond, Giachetti, and Marosi 2009:97–105. These structures were originally designated by Reich as "Room A" and "Room B": Houston 1978:5–7; Rowe 1979:17–20.

3. Investigated especially by Tracchi (1978:17, 19). No excavations have been carried out here by Florida State University.

4. For example at Marcianella near Chiusi: Pucci and Mascione 2003, Olcese 2012:101–107; and Podere Funghi near Poggio Colla (Vicchio): Warden et al. 2005: 258–262, Olcese 2012:50.

5. De Grummond 2000: pl. 52a and b.

6. Houston 1978.

7. Colonna and de Grummond 2007. De Grummond, Giachetti, and Marosi 2009:159–164. Bagnasco Gianni 2014a.

8. Giovanni Colonna favors this interpretation: Colonna and de Grummond 2007.

9. Bagnasco Gianni 2014a. Though the ligature was published in *REE* of *Studi Etruschi* as early as Robertson 1989, it is not recognized as a word in Rix and Meiser 2014.

10. Fundamental is de Grummond, Giachetti, and Marosi 2009:39–96. See also de Grummond 2017:171–181.

11. Note the categories discussed by Edlund-Berry (2011:9).

12. Cf. the Belvedere temple at Orvieto and Pyrgi Temples A and B: Colonna 1985:81–82 and 129.

13. Cf. Building Delta, Courtyard T, the sacred area of Adonis at Gravisca: Fiorini 2005:95–96.

14. Tracchi 1978:17.

15. Prayon 1991:1289, fig. 1.

16. Prayon 1991:1289. Oriented to the southeast were the Belvedere temple of Orvieto (sacred to Tinia) and the Portonaccio temple at Veii (sacred perhaps to Menerva). The Cannicella sanctuary at Orvieto (sacred to the goddess Vei) was likely also oriented to the southeast. The temple at Punta della Vipera (sacred to Menerva) and Temple B at Pyrgi (sacred to Uni) were both oriented toward the southwest. The recently discovered temple to Tin(i)a at Marzabotto is oriented exactly north to south: Sassatelli and Govi 2010.

17. De Grummond, Giachetti, and Marosi 2009:40.

18. Especially interesting is the cavity at Pian di Civita at Tarquinia, almost certainly connected with prophecy: Bonghi Jovino and Chiaramonte Treré 1997:217–220 and de Grummond 2016:153–159.

19. For full details of the votive features see De Grummond, Giachetti, and Marosi 2009:45–92.

20. Discussion of nails in cult in de Grummond 2007; de Grummond, Giachetti, and Marosi 2009:41–43. Sacred nails from Fontanile di Legnisina, Vulci: Ricciardi 1988–1989:195–197.

21. De Grummond, Giachetti, and Marosi 2009:56 (cat. no. 16, silver clad coin), 63 (cat. no. 35, black-gloss saucer).

22. Colonna (2006:132–135) discusses similar rubble altars at Pyrgi.

23. De Grummond 1985:36; de Grummond 1991:58, 61–63.

24. Harris 1971:251–263.

CHAPTER 5. THE WELLS OF CETAMURA

1. De Grummond 2017 for a full account. Also relevant are de Grummond 1985; de Grummond, Rowe, Ewell, and Bizzarri 1999; de Grummond, Sowder, Cini et al. 2015; de Grummond, Sowder, Marosi et al. 2015.

2. De Grummond 2017:180–181, cat. no. 174 (with A. V. Ryals). Bentz 1992:53 (from the temple at Fiesole), 95–96 (from Arezzo and Siena).

3. Giachi 2017.

4. Slight differences in the listing of the number and identification of taxa occurred as research proceeded, in part when the oaks were listed separately. For the most authoritative and up-to-date overview, upon which this listing is based, see Mariotti Lippi et al., under review.

5. De Grummond 2017:67–79.

6. De Grummond 2017:78–79 (cat. no. 21).

7. Colonna 1992:117.

8. For the architecture of the wells, see Sowder 2017.

9. See most recently Holland 2017 as well as Chellini 2002, *Aqua degli dei*, and Giontella 2012.

10. De Grummond 2017:121 (cat. nos. 83–84), 161–162 (cat. nos. 146–147), and 220–222 (cat. nos. 226–229) (all entries by C. L. Sowder and M. Romano).

11. De Grummond, Sowder, Cini et al. 2015; Sowder 2015; de Grummond 2017:112–118.

12. Romualdi 1998:16 and 2000:362–363, for an example from Populonia.

13. Sowder 2015:164. Skylla figure: Cianferoni 1992:25, figs. 35–36. Guilloche decoration: Romualdi 1998:17.

14. Maggiani 2003:40–41; Sowder 2015:161–162; Holland 2017:51–54.

15. Studied by A. V. Ryals: de Grummond 2017:89–93 (introduction by Ryals and de Grummond; cat. nos. 38–48; entries by Ryals).

16. Studied by K. Slusher: de Grummond 2017:83–88 (introduction by Slusher and de Grummond; cat. nos. 24–37; entries by Slusher).

17. Original analysis by O. Fonzo; cultural research and interpretation by L. Holland and P. Lebo in de Grummond 2017:81–82 (introduction by Holland and Lebo; cat. no. 23; entry by Holland and Lebo).

18. Studied by C. Cha: Grummond 2017:138–143 (introduction by Cha and de Grummond; cat. nos. 111–118; entries by Cha).

19. Mariotti Lippi and Mori Secci 2017.

20. Castiglioni, Cottini, and Rottoli 2017.

21. Corbino and Fonzo 2017.

22. Corbino and Fonzo 2017.

CHAPTER 6. ROMAN CETAMURA

1. De Grummond 2017:236–243(introduction by L. Taylor; cat. nos. 249–266; entries by Taylor with C. Russo and H. Wink), and appendix C, "Handlist of Terra Sigillata Stamps from Cetamura," 349–351 (Taylor and de Grummond). For C. Septimius, see OCK, 1872 and de Grummond 2017:237 (cat. no. 249).

2. De Grummond 2017:166–167 (cat. no. 155; entry by C. L. Sowder). See Giuliani-Pomes 1954:155–166, for other Etruscan examples.

3. De Grummond 2000:12–15 (by P. Rowe). De Grummond 2017:208–210 (by L. Taylor).

4. De Grummond 2017:248–251 (by L. Holland).

5. Coin of Antony: Crawford RRC 489/3; de Grummond 2017:200–201 (cat. no. 200; entry by M. Dempsey and L. Holland). Stamp of Anteros: OCK, 372. De Grummond 2017:211 (cat. no. 210; entry by L. Taylor and H. Wink).

6. Corbino and de Grummond 2016.

7. De Grummond 2017:220–222 (cat. nos. 226–230; entries by C. L. Sowder and M. Romano).

8. MMI: De Grummond, 2017:237 (cat. no. 251; entry by L. Taylor with C. Russo and H. Wink).

9. De Grummond 2017:224 (cat. no. 231; entry by L. Taylor).

10. De Grummond 2017:222 (cat. no. 229; entry by C. L. Sowder).

11. De Grummond 2017:162 (cat. no. 147; entry by C. L. Sowder and M. Romano).

12. See note 1 above for references to these stamps.

13. De Grummond 2000:38 (cat. nos. 138–139). De Grummond 2017:244–247 (introduction and entries cat. nos. 267–272 by L. Holland).

14. De Grummond, Giachetti, and Marosi 2009:137–140 (esp. cat. nos. 165–172, including specimens for shipping, wine [mostly], oil, and garum).

15. De Grummond 2000:36–37 (cat. nos. 125–137); de Grummond 2017:215–218 (introduction by J. Samuels; cat. nos. 218–223; entries by L. Taylor and de Grummond).

16. De Grummond 2017:226–231 (cat. nos. 234–240; entries by de Grummond, L. Holland, C. L. Sowder, and C. A. Ewell; cat. no. 240 is the pitcher and the rest are situlae).

17. Tassinari 1993, with many comparanda (types X1612 and X1622).

18. De Grummond 2017:234 (cat. no. 246; entry by C. A. Ewell). Some of the lead feet found separated from their buckets were subsequently reattached during conservation (cat. nos. 234–235, 237–239).

19. De Grummond 2017:225 (cat. no. 233; entry by L. Holland).

20. De Grummond 2017:155 (cat. no. 136; entry by L. Holland).

21. De Grummond 2017:149–153 (introduction and entries by K. Swanson and L. Holland; cat. nos. 124–133), for bone implements from Cetamura, many of which were found lower down in the transitional section (Well Group IV). The needle, cat. no. 124, and broken implement, cat. no. 133, were the only ones found at a clearly Roman level.

22. De Grummond, Sowder, Cini et al. 2015:368, fig. 6.

23. Mariotti Lippi and Mori Secci 2017:313–314.

24. Mariotti Lippi and Mori Secci 2017:318–320.

25. De Grummond 2017:219 (cat. no. 224; entry by C. L. Sowder). Katzev (1969: 57) published Greek hopper-type grain mills of the fourth century BCE that have a similar V-shaped depression and perforation. These have grooves on top to brace a handle that would be used to rotate the mill back and forth, a feature that is lacking on the Cetamura piece.

26. Traccchi 1978:16. See also de Grummond 1984; de Grummond, Rowe, Marrinan, and Doran 1994:93–94; de Grummond 2000:11.

27. Bartolozzi wrote a report, with drawing, for Tracchi: de Grummond 2017: appendix A, 339–345.

28. For the restored wellhead and capstone see Sowder 2017:32; de Grummond 2017:63–66 (cat. nos. 1–4; entries by C. L. Sowder).

29. Marzabotto: Mansuelli et al. 1982:90, Region IV, Insula 1, House 6 (ca. 500 BCE), squared wellhead with circular opening. Vetulonia: Cecconi 1978:20, half of a drain or wellhead (third–second century BCE).

30. Dupondius of Trajan discovered by J. Oleson in 1976 near the fortification wall separating Zone I from Zone II, unpublished. Coin of Marcus Aurelius: Tracchi 1978:20.

31. Pitchers: De Grummond 2017:256 (cat. nos. 283–284, third–fourth cen-

tury CE, with close comparanda from Volterra). Fabric with wavy lines: de Grummond 2017:256 (cat. nos. 285–286).

CHAPTER 7. CETAMURA AS A COMMUNITY

1. Cetamura, at 695 masl, is actually on higher ground than Volterra (552 masl), Arezzo (296 masl), Fiesole (295 masl), and Chiusi (348 masl) as well as Caere (81 masl) and Veii (105 masl).

2. See, for example, V. Bellelli, in de Grummond and Pieraccini 2016:57, note 3, on estimates that Caere surely had thousands, perhaps as many as one hundred thousand, at its peak.

3. E.g., Bellelli in de Grummond and Pieraccini 2016: figs. 5.4, 5.5. Pulcinelli 2019: fig. 17.4.

4. Valenti 1995:253 (no. 182) refers to Cetamura as both *fortezza d'altura* and *oppidum*. Becker (2002) calls it a *castellum*. See Becker's thoughtful discussion of the different terms that may be used for small Etruscan settlements.

5. Becker 2002:89.

6. See Bizzarri and Soren 2016:136–145 for recent case studies and essential bibliography.

7. See the recent succinct characterization in Tuck 2016:108 and the relevant bibliography 114–115.

8. See most recently Marcone 2017:1197, which mentions the possibility of slave ownership of workshops.

9. See the list of all Arretine stamps from Cetamura known at present: de Grummond 2017:349–351.

10. E.g., Maras 2009:349–356 (Caere: Uni at the port of Pyrgi); Bagnasco Gianni 2014b (Tarquinia: Uni at Pian di Civita); Maras 2009:251–252 (Cortona: Uni and Tinia). The case should not be overstated, since they also appear in many sacred places outside the major cities.

11. Maras 2009:223–224.

12. Belelli Marchesini 2019.

13. Maggiani 2016; Warden 2016.

14. De Grummond 2014b:143.

CHAPTER 8. CETAMURA AFTER ANTIQUITY

1. Pagliai 2008:32 (doc. 61), 141–142 (doc. 309), 146 (doc. 319), 163 (doc. 361). De Grummond 2000:10 reviews these documents. Several corrections have since been made to the interpretations given there. The "Timeline of History for Cetamura del Chianti" (below) incorporates the latest views.

2. Boglione (1993:47–48) first published this document.

3. Rowe (2000:15–17) reviews the architecture of the medieval component of Cetamura as known at the time of that publication. Recent developments in 2016–2018 in the medieval structures next to Well #1 are as yet unpublished.

4. Cimarri 2009.

5. Tracchi (1978:15–21) does not in fact give the date of the discovery. Reich (1973:17) reports the date, evidently obtained personally from Tracchi, as September 12, 1964. Silvana Tracchi, widow of the archaeologist, recently commented to N. de Grummond that he may have already visited the site in 1958.

6. Reich 1972.

7. Cini, Cecchini, and Violetti 2017.

8. Giachetti and Marosi 2009; Marosi 2017.

9. Giachi 2017; Mori Secci 2009; Mariotti Lippi and Mori Secci 2017; Cottini 2009; Castiglioni, Cottini, and Rottoli 2017.

10. Corbino and de Grummond 2016; Fonzo and de Grummond 2016; Corbino and Fonzo 2017.

11. Bouby, Ivorra, and Terral 2017; Wales, Ramos-Madrigal, and Gilbert 2017.

12. Aversano et al. 2017.

13. De Grummond 2018b.

14. Ciacci, Rendini, and Zifferero 2012 is among the richest of new publications. See also de Grummond 2018b, esp. notes 17–18 for relevant references.

REFERENCES

Acqua degli dei = *L'acqua degli dei, immagini di fontane, vasellame, culti salutari e in grotto* (exh. cat.) (Montepulciano, 2003).

Archeologia urbana a Fiesole = *Archeologia urbana a Fiesole: Lo scavo di Via Marini–Via Portigiani* (Florence, 1990).

Ascheri, M., and V. De Dominicis, eds. 1997. *Tra Siena e il Vescovado: L'area della Selva. Beni culturali, ambientali e storici di un territorio*. Siena.

Atlante Toscana = *Atlante dei siti archeologici della Toscana*, ed. M. Torelli et al. (Florence, 1992).

Aversano, R., B. Basile, M. P. Buonincontri, F. Carrucci, D. Carputo, L. Frusciante, and Gaetano Di Pasquale. 2017. "Dating the Beginning of the Roman Viticultural Model in the Western Mediterranean: The Case Study of Chianti (Central Italy)." PLOS ONE November 15, 2017: http://journals.plos.org/plosone/article?id=10.1371/journal.pone.0186298.

Bagnasco Gianni, G. 2014a. "At First Glance: Remarks on a Group of Sigla from the Sanctuary of the Etruscan Artisans at Cetamura del Chianti." *EtrStud* 17: 192–212.

———. 2014b. "Una nuova iscrizione dal 'Complesso Monumentale' della Civita di Tarquinia." In *Per Maristella Pandolfini, cên zic ziχuχe*, ed. E. Benelli, 23–28. *Mediterranea* Suppl. 10. Pisa.

Bagnasco Gianni, G., and N. T. de Grummond. Forthcoming. "The International Etruscan Sigla Project: An Introduction." In *Etruscan Literacy in Its Social Context*, ed. K. Lomas, R. Whitehouse, and J. Wilkins. London.

Becker, H. 2002. "The Etruscan Castellum: Fortified Settlements and Regional Autonomy in Etruria." *EtrStud* 9:85–95.

———. 2017. "Economy, 580–450 BCE." In Naso 2017:1013–1029.

Belelli Marchesini, B. 2019. "Kilns and Evidence of Ceramic Production." In Tabolli 2019:201–206.

Bell, S., and A. A. Carpino, eds. 2016. *A Companion to the Etruscans.* Wiley-Blackwell.

Bentz, M. 1992. *Etruskische Votivbronzen des Hellenismus. Biblioteca di StEtr* 25. Florence.

Bizzarri, C., and D. Soren. 2016. "Etruscan Domestic Architecture, Hydraulic Engineering, and Water Management Technologies." In Bell and Carpino 2016: 129–145.

Bocci, P. 1965. "Catalogo della ceramica di Roselle." *StEtr* 33:109–190.

Boglione, A. 1993. "Montegrossi tra l'Impero e il Comune di Firenze." In *Montegrossoli e Semifonte: Due capisaldi della politica imperiale nella Toscana del XII secolo,* 25–47. Radda.

Bonfante, L., ed. 1986a. *Etruscan Life and Afterlife: A Handbook of Etruscan Studies.* Detroit.

———. 1986b. "Introduction: Etruscan Studies Today." In Bonfante 1986a:1–17.

Bonghi Jovino, M. 2005. "*Mini muluvanice—mini turuce*: Depositi votivi e sacralità dall'analisi del rituale alla lettura interpretativa delle forme di religiosità." In *Depositi votivi e culti dell'Italia antica dall'età arcaica a quella tardo-repubblicana,* ed. A. Comella and S. Mele, 31–46. Bari.

Bonghi Jovino, M., and C. Chiaramonte Treré, eds. 1997. *Tarquinia: Testimonianze archeologiche e ricostruzione storica. Scavi sistematici nell'abitato, 1982–1988. Tarchna* 1. Rome.

Bon-Harper, S. 2011. "Investigating Etruscan Ceramic Production at the Podere Funghi." *EtrStud* 14:125–140.

Bouby, L., S. Ivorra, and J.-F. Terral. 2017. "Morphometric Analysis of Vitis Seeds from Well #1 at Cetamura del Chianti: First Results." In de Grummond 2017: 289–293.

Camporeale, G. 2009. "Arezzo in età etrusca: Profilo storico." In *Arezzo nell'antichità,* ed. G. Camporeale and G. Firpo, 55–82. Rome.

Castiglioni, E., M. Cottini, and M. Rottoli. 2017. "Nuts, Seeds, Wood, and Charcoals from the Wells and from Structure K at Cetamura del Chianti (SI)." In de Grummond 2017:271–288.

Cavallo, D. 1992. *Via Cassia* 1: *Via Cimina.* Rome.

Ceccarelli, L. 2016. "The Romanization of Etruria." In Bell and Carpino 2016:28–40.

Cecconi, V. 1978. *Profilo di una città etrusca: Vetulonia.* Pistoia.

Cha, C. 2015. "Ceramic Weights from the Well at Cetamura del Chianti." MA thesis, Florida State University, Tallahassee.

Chellini, R. 2002. *Acque sorgive salutari e sacre in Etruria (Italiae Regio VII): Ricerche archeologiche e di topografia antica.* Oxford.

Ciacci, A., P. Rendini, and A. Zifferero, eds. 2012. *Archeologia della vite e del vino in Toscana e nel Lazio: Dalle techniche dell'indagine archeologica alle prospettive della biologia moleculare.* Florence.

Cianferoni, G. C. 1984. *San Martino ai Colli: Un centro rurale etrusco in Val d'Elsa.* Rome.

———. 1992. "I reperti metallici." In *Populonia in età ellenistica: I materiali dalle necropoli*, ed. A. Romualdi, 13–41. Florence.

———. 2001. *Siena, Museo Archeologico, Santa Maria della Scala.* Siena.

———, ed. 2012. *Vino: Fra mito e storia. Catalogo della mostra. Siena 24 novembre 2012–5 maggio, 2013.* Monteriggioni.

Cimarri, V. 2009. "The Middle Ages at Cetamura." In de Grummond, Giachetti, and Marosi 2009:147–152.

Cini, F., L. Cecchini, and A. Violetti. 2017. "Excavation Methodology." In de Grummond 2017:36–42.

Colonna, G., ed. 1985. *Santuari d'Etruria.* Milan.

———. 1992. "Gli oggetti lignei." In *Pyrgi: Scavi del santuario etrusco (1969–1971)*, 111–121. II Suppl. to *NSc* 42–43 (1988–1989).

———. 2006. "Sacred Architecture and the Religion of the Etruscans." In *The Religion of the Etruscans*, ed. N. T. de Grummond and E. Simon, 132–168. Austin.

Colonna, G., and N. T. de Grummond. 2007. "Ager Saenensis: Cetamura del Chianti (Gaiole in Chianti)." In *Rivista di Epigrafia Etrusca. StEtr* 73:302–307.

Corbino, C. A., and N. T. de Grummond. 2016. "I volatili allevati a Cetamura del Chianti (I sec. d.C.) / Breeding of Birds at Cetamura del Chianti (1st century A.D.)." *Atti del 7º Convegno Nazionale di Archeozoologia. Annali dell'Università degli Studi di Ferrara* 12:225–232.

Corbino, C. A., and O. Fonzo. 2017. "The Use of Animals in Etruscan and Roman Rituals at Cetamura del Chianti (SI)." In de Grummond 2017:323–335.

Cottini, M. 2009. "Archaeobotanical Analysis in Zone II." In de Grummond, Giachetti, and Marosi 2009:175–187.

Cresci, M., and L. Viviani. 1995. "Defining an Economic Area of the Hellenistic Period in Inland Northern Etruria: The Excavation of a Fortified Hilltop Village at Poggio La Croce in Radda in Chianti." *EtrStud* 2:141–157.

Cresci, M., et al. 1995. "Poggio La Croce–Radda in Chianti: Rapporto preliminare delle campagne di scavo 1989–1992." In Valenti 1995:260–285.

Cristofani, M. 1979. *Siena: Le origini, testimonianze e miti archeologici* (exh. cat.). Florence.

Cristofani, M., and M. Cristofani-Martelli. 1972. "Ceramica presigillata da Volterra." *MÉFRA* 84:499–514.

Cuomo di Caprio, N. 1985. *La ceramica in archeologia: Antiche tecniche di lavorazione e moderni metodi d'indagine.* Rome.

Curri, C., and S. Sorbelli. 1973. "Note sulla tecnologia delle officine ceramiche etrusche e della scuola coroplastica di Veio." *StEtr* 41:245–266.

Curry, Jill. 1996. "Black-Gloss Pottery from the Kiln Area at Cetamura del Chianti, Italy." MA thesis, Florida State University, Tallahassee.

Davis, D., and R. Kortum. 2014. "The *Nuovo Forno Etrusco*: An Etruscan Kiln Project." *EtrStud* 17:233–266.

de Grummond, N. T. 1985. "Excavations at Cetamura del Chianti, 1983–84." *ArchNews* 14:29–38.

———. 1991. "The Etruscan Settlement at Cetamura del Chianti." In *Gli etruschi nel Chianti. Il Chianti: Storia, arte, cultura territorio* 15:49–68.

———, ed. 2000. *Cetamura Antica: Traditions of Chianti*. Tallahassee. [Italian translation by A. Frascarelli, *Cetamura Antica: Tradizioni del Chianti* (Orvieto, 2000).]

———. 2001. "The Cult of the Kiln." *Archaeology* 54 (Jan.–Feb.), 58–60.

———. 2005. "Sestius at Cetamura and Lurius at Cosa?" In J. Pollini, ed., *Terra marique: Studies in Honor of Anna Marguerite McCann*, 30–39. Oxford.

———. 2008. "Gaiole in Chianti (SI): Scavi nel Santuario degli Artigiani Etruschi a Cetamura del Chianti (Civitamura), 2007–2008." *Notiziario della Soprintendenza per i Beni Archeologici della Toscana* 4:446–451.

———. 2010. "A Scarab Gem from the Etruscan Artisans' Quarter and Sacred Area at Cetamura del Chianti." *Rasenna: Journal of the Center for Etruscan Studies*. http://scholarworks.umass.edu/rasenna/.

———. 2011. "Ritual Practices at the Sanctuary of the Etruscan Artisans at Cetamura del Chianti." In de Grummond and Edlund Berry 2011:68–88.

———. 2014a. "Cetamura." In Firmati 2014:113–115.

———. 2014b. "The Cult of Lur: Prophecy and Human Sacrifice?" In *Studi e ricerche a Tarquinia e in Etruria. Atti del simposio internazionale in ricordo di Francesca Romana Serra Ridgway, Tarquinia 24–25 settembre 2010*, ed. M. D. Gentili and L. Maneschi, 141–152. *Mediterranea* 11. Rome.

———. 2015. "Holy Waters at Cetamura." *Etruscan News* 17:6–7.

———. 2016. "Etruscan Human Sacrifice: The Case of Tarquinia." *Diversity of Sacrifice: Form and Function of Sacrificial Practices in the Ancient World and Beyond*, ed. C. A. Murray, 145–168. Albany.

———, ed. 2017. *Wells of Wonders: New Discoveries at Cetamura del Chianti. Catalog of the Exhibition, June 9–September 30, 2017*. Florence.

———. 2018a. "The Curious Case of Castellina in Chianti and Evidence for the Reception of Etruscan Culture in Sixteenth-Century Europe." In *An Etruscan Affair: The Impact of Early Etruscan Discoveries on European Culture*, ed. Judith Swaddling, 113–122. London.

———. 2018b. "Grape Pips from Etruscan and Roman Cetamura del Chianti: On Stratigraphy, Literary Sources, and Pruning Hooks." *EtrStud* 21:27–57.

de Grummond, N. T., C. Bare, and A. Meilleur. 2000. "Etruscan Sigla ('Graffiti'): Prolegomena and Some Case Studies." *Archaeologia Transatlantica* 18:25–38.

de Grummond, N. T., and I. Edlund-Berry, eds. 2011. *The Archaeology of Sanctuaries and Ritual in Etruria*. *JRA* Suppl. 81.

de Grummond, N. T., R. Giachetti, and N. Marosi, eds. 2009. *The Sanctuary of the Etruscan Artisans at Cetamura del Chianti: The Legacy of Alvaro Tracchi*. Florence.

de Grummond, N. T., and L. Pieraccini, eds. 2016. *Caere*. Austin.

de Grummond, N. T., and H. Rix. 1985. "Ager Saenensis, Cetamura in Chianti: LAUSINI." In *Rivista di Epigrafia Etrusca, StEtr*, 52: 276–277.

de Grummond, N. T., P. Rowe, C. Ewell, and C. Bizzarri. 1999. "Excavations at Cetamura del Chianti (Civitamura), 1992–1998: Preliminary Report." *EtrStud* 6:163–184.

de Grummond, N. T., P. Rowe, R. Marrinan, and G. Doran. 1994. "Excavations at Cetamura del Chianti, 1987–91." *EtrStud* 1:84–122.

de Grummond, N. T., C. Sowder, F. Cini, L. Holland, L. Cecchini, M. Romano, A. Violetti, and N. Marosi. 2015. "Gaiole in Chianti (SI): Scavo del pozzo etrusco a Cetamura del Chianti, 2011–2014." *Notiziario della Soprintendenza per i beni Archeologici della Toscana* 11:366–374.

de Grummond, N. T., C. Sowder, N. Marosi, L. Cecchini, and F. Cini. 2015. "Excavations in an Etruscan Well at Cetamura del Chianti: A Preliminary Report." *EtrStud* 18:3–27.

Edlund-Berry, I. 2011. "Introduction." In de Grummond and Edlund-Berry 2011: 7–15.

Ewell, C. 2014. "The Kiln at Cetamura del Chianti." *EtrStud* 17:213–232.

Fiorini, L. 2005. *Gravisca: Scavi nel santuario greco 1.1: Topografia generale e storia del santuario: Analisi dei contesti e delle stratigrafie*. Bari.

Firmati, M., ed. 2014. *Castellina in Chianti, Archaeological Museum of the Sienese Chianti*. Milan.

Fonzo, O., and N. T. de Grummond. "Resti di Mammiferi domestici in contesto romano-imperiale: Il caso di Cetamura del Chianti (I sec. d.C.) / Remains of Domestic Mammals from an Imperial Roman Context: Cetamura del Chianti (1st century A.D.)." *Atti del 7° Convegno Nazionale di Archeozoologia. Annali dell'Università degli Studi di Ferrara* 12:219–224.

Giachetti, R., and N. Marosi. 2009. "Conservation and Restoration of Objects from Cetamura by Studio Art Centers International (SACI)." In de Grummond, Giachetti, and Marosi 2009:167–174.

Giachi, G. 2017. "Wood from Well #1 at Cetamura del Chianti (SI)." In de Grummond 2017:303–310.

Giontella, C. 2012. *"Nullus enim fons non sacer": Cult idrici di epoca preromana e romana (Regiones VI–VII)*. Pisa.

Giroldini, P. 2017. "The Etruscans in Chianti." In de Grummond 2017:19–30.

Giuliani-Pomes, M. V. 1954. "Cronologia delle situle rinvenute in Etruria." *StEtr* 23:149–194.

Goggioli, S. 2012. "Lo scavo di Bosco Le Pici." In Cianferoni 2012:134–138.

Hackworth, L. 1993. "Evidence of Textile Production at Cetamura del Chianti, Italy: A Catalog and a Context." MA thesis, Florida State University, Tallahassee.

Hansson, Ulf. 2002. "Gemma a scarabeo." *Castiglion Fiorentino, Tesori ritrovati: Reperti archeologici etruschi rinvenuti nel territorio di Castiglion Fiorentino dal sec. XVIII ad oggi*, ed. P. Zamarchi Grasse and M. Scarpellini, 33–34. Montepulciano.

———. 2005. *A Globolo Gems: Late Etrusco-Italic Scarab Intaglios*. Göteborg.

Hargis, M. 2007. "A Mortarium at Cetamura del Chianti in Context." MA thesis, Florida State University, Tallahassee.

Harris, W. V. 1971. *Rome in Etruria and Umbria*. Oxford.

Hayes, J. 1984. *Greek and Italian Black-Gloss Wares in the Royal Ontario Museum: A Catalogue*. Toronto.

Haynes, S. 2000. *Etruscan Civilization: A Cultural History*. Los Angeles.

Holland, L. 2017. "Water and Rituals at Cetamura." In de Grummond 2017:51–57.

Houston, M. 1978. "Cetamura Black-Glaze Pottery." MA thesis, Florida State University, Tallahassee.

Jolivet, V. 2014. "A Long Twilight (396–90 BC): Romanization of Etruria." In Turfa 2014:151–179.

Katzev, M. L. 1969. "The Kyrenia Shipwreck." *Expedition Magazine* 11.2:55–59.

Layton, S. A. 2009. "Etruscan Bucchero Pottery from Cetamura del Chianti." *EtrStud* 12:21–60.

Ling, R. 1988. "Hellenistic and Graeco-Roman Art." In *Greece and the Hellenistic World*, ed. J. Boardman, J. Griffin, and O. Murray, 380–408. Oxford.

Maggiani, A. 2003. "Acque 'sante' in Etruria." In *Acqua degli dei*, 39–43.

———. 2016. "The Vicchio Stele: The Inscription." *EtrStud* 19:220–224.

Mangani, E. 1985. "Castelnuovo Berardenga." In *Case e palazzi d'Etruria*, ed. S. Stopponi, 155–163. Milan.

———. 1986. *I centri archeologici della provincia di Siena*. Siena.

———. 1988–1989. "Castelnuovo Berardenga (Siena): L'orientalizzante recente in Etruria settentrionale: Tomba A della necropoli principesca del Poggione (1980)." *NSc* 42–43:5–84.

Mansuelli, G., A. M. Brizzolara, S. De Maria, G. Sassatelli, and D. Vitali. 1982. *Guida alla città etrusca e al museo di Marzabotto*. Bologna.

Maras, D. 2009. *Il dono votivo: Gli dei e il sacro nelle iscrizioni etrusche di culto*. Pisa.

Marcone, A. 2017. "Society, 250–89 BCE." In Naso 2017:2.1191–1201.

Mariotti Lippi, M., and M. Mori Secci. 2017. "Palynological Analysis in Well #1 of Cetamura del Chianti (SI)." In de Grummond 2017:311–321.

Mariotti Lippi, M., M. Mori Secci, G. Giachi, L. Bouby, J.-F. Terral, E. Castiglioni, M. Cottini, M. Rottoli, and N. de Grummond. Under review. "Plant Remains in an Etruscan-Roman Well at Cetamura del Chianti, Italy."

Marosi, N. 2017. "Conserving Wonders: Conservation-Restoration Work by Students of SACI." In de Grummond 2017:10–11.

Martelli, M. 1981. "Scavo di edifici nella zona industriale di Populonia." In *L'Etruria mineraria. Atti del XII Convegno di Studi Etruschi ed Italici*, 161–172. Florence.

Milani, L. A. 1905. "Montecalvario: Ipogeo paleoetrusco di Montecalvario presso Castellina in Chianti." *NSc* 2:223–242.

Mori Secci, M. 2009. "Chickpeas at Cetamura in Votive Feature 7: Archaeobotanical Results from a Cooking Pot (Cat. No. 94)." In de Grummond, Giachetti, and Marosi 2009:189–190.

Naso, A., ed. 2017. *Etruscology*. 2 vols. Boston.

OCK = A. Oxé and H. Comfort, eds., rev. and enl. P. Kenrick. *Corpus Vasorum Arretinorum, A Catalogue of the Signatures, Shapes and Chronology of Italian Sigillata* (Bonn, 2000).

Olcese, G., ed. 2012. *Atlante dei siti di produzione ceramica (Toscana, Lazio, Campania e Sicilia) . . . IV secolo a.C.–I secolo d.C.* Rome.

Osmond, J. K. 1994. "The Geology and Hydrology of Cetamura del Chianti." *EtrStud* 1:116–122.

Pagliai, D. L. 2008. *Regesto di Coltibuono*. Fonti per la storia del Chianti 3. Florence.

Pasqui, A. 1997. "Il passato più remoto." In Ascheri and De Dominicis 1997:38–116.

Pecci, A., and M. A. Cau Ontiveros. 2017. "Results of Analysis of Residues in a Ceramic Vessel (C-10-634), from Cetamura del Chianti (SI)." In de Grummond 2017:267–270.

Peña, J. T. 1990. "Internal Red-Slip Cookware (Pompeian Red Ware) from Cetamura del Chianti, Italy: Mineralogical Composition and Provenience." *AJA* 94: 647–661.

Peña, J. T., and S. Gallimore. 2014. "Black-Gloss Ware, North Etrurian Red-Slip Ware, and Italian Terra Sigillata from Cetamura del Chianti: Composition, Provenance, Supply, and Consumption." *HEROM: Journal on Hellenistic and Roman Culture* 3:72–224.

Pericci, F., ed. 2018. *Carta archeologica della provincia di Siena, 13: Monteroni d'Arbia*. Siena.

Pernier, L. 1916. "Montecalvario, presso Castellina in Chianti: Grande tumulo con ipogei paleoetruschi sul poggio di Montecalvario." *NSc* 1916:263–281.

Pianu, G. 2000. *Gravisca, scavi nel santuario greco 2: Il bucchero*. Bari.

Prayon, F. 1991. "Deorum sedes: Sull'Orientamento dei templi etrusco-italici." In *Miscellanea etrusca e italica in onore di Massimo Pallottino*, ed. G. Colonna and R. A. Staccioli. *ArchCl* 43:1285–1295.

Price, S. 1988. "The History of the Hellenistic Period." In *Greece and the Hellenistic World*, ed. J. Boardman, J. Griffin, and O. Murray, 309–331. Oxford.

Pucci, G., and C. Mascione, eds. 2003. *Manifattura ceramica etrusco-romana a Chiusi: Il complesso produttivo di Marcianella*. Bari.

Pulcinelli, L. 2019. "The Defensive System." In Tabolli 2019:147–153.

Rasmussen, T. 1979. *Bucchero Pottery from Southern Etruria*. Cambridge.

Reich, J. J. 1972. "Cetamura (Cetramura): Excavation of an Etruscan Settlement." *ArchNews* 1:14–17.

———. 1973. "Cetramura (Cetamura): Further Observations." *ArchNews* 2:17–20.

———. 1980. "Excavations at Cetamura: Recent Developments." *ArchNews* 9:57–60.

Ricciardi, L. 1988–1989. "Il santuario etrusco di Fontanile di Legnisina: Relazione delle campagne di scavo 1985 e 1986: L'altare monumentale e il deposito votivo." *NSc* 42–43:137–209.

Rix, H., and G. Meiser. 2014. *Etruskische Texte: Editio minor*. Tübingen.

Robertson, M. 1989. "Cetamura del Chianti." In *Rivista di Epigrafia Etrusca. StEtr* 55:279–309.

Rolfo, M. F. 2009. "Lithics." In de Grummond, Giachetti, and Marosi 2009:153–155.

Romualdi, A. 1993. *Populonia e il suo territorio: Profilo storico-archeologico*. Florence.

———. 1998. *Una donna di rango a Populonia: Tra la fine del quinto e gli inizi del quarto secolo a.C.* Florence.

———. 2000. "La tomba delle hydriai di Meidias." *Ostraka* 9:351–371.

Rowe, P. 1979. "Excavations at Cetamura: A Study of Architecture." MA thesis, Florida State University, Tallahassee.

———. 2000. "Zone I, Area G: The Roman Baths" and "Zone I, Area G: The Post-Classical Structures." In de Grummond 2000:12–17.

Sassatelli, G., and E. Govi. 2010. "Cults and Foundation Rites in the Etruscan City of Marzabotto." In *Material Aspects of Etruscan Religion*, ed. L. B. van der Meer, 17–27. *BABesch* Suppl. 16. Leuven.

Sowder, C. L. 1978. "A Preliminary Classification of the Utilitarian Pottery at Cetamura." MA thesis, Florida State University, Tallahassee.

———. 1984. "Utilitarian Pottery from Cetamura del Chianti." *ArchNews* 13:13–25.

———. 2015. "Religion and Industry at Cetamura del Chianti in the Late Etruscan Period: The Well." *EtrStud* 18:151–177.

———. 2017. "Architecture of the Wells." In de Grummond 2017:31–35.

Tabolli, J., ed. 2019. *Veii*. Austin.

Tassinari, S. 1993. *Il vasellame bronzeo di Pompeii*. 2 vols. Rome.

Taylor, L. 2014. "Preface and Introduction." *EtrStud* 17:111–120.

———. 2015. "Religion and Industry at Cetamura del Chianti in the Late Etruscan Period: The Artisans' Quarter." *EtrStud* 18:126–150.

Torelli, M. 1986. "History: Land and People." In Bonfante 1986:47–65.

Tracchi, A. 1966. "Ritrovamenti sulle colline Chianti-Valdarno." *StEtr* 34:287–293.

———. 1971. "Di alcune antiche strade dell'Etruria settentrionale." *L'Universo* 51: 339–368.

———. 1978. *Dal Chianti al Valdarno*. Rome.

Tuck, A. 2009. "Core and Periphery in Inland Etruria: Poggio Civitate and the Etruscan Settlement in Vescovado di Murlo." *EtrStud* 12:215–237.

———. 2016. "Poggio Civitate: Community Form in Inland Etruria." In Bell and Carpino 2016:105–116.

Turfa, J. M. 2014. *The Etruscan World*. London.

Valenti, M. 1995. *Carta archeologica della provincia di Siena, 1: Il Chianti senese*. Siena.

Wales, N., J. Ramos-Madrigal, and M. T. P. Gilbert. 2017. "Ancient DNA Analysis of Vitis Seeds from Cetamura del Chianti: Current Results." In de Grummond 2017:294–302.

Warden, P. G. 2016. "The Vicchio Stele and Its Context." *EtrStud* 19:208–219.

Warden, P. G., M. L. Thomas, A. Steiner, and G. Meyers. 2005. "Poggio Colla: A North Etruscan Settlement of the 7th–2nd C. B.C. (1998–2004 Excavations)." *JRA* 18:252–266.

Wilkens, B. 2009. "Faunal Remains from the Refuse Pits 1 and 2 (RP 1 and 2) at Cetamura." In de Grummond, Giachetti, and Marosi 2009:195–204.

Williams, F. 1996. "Red Gloss Pottery from Cetamura del Chianti (1973–1991)." MA thesis, Florida State University, Tallahassee.

Wiman, I. M. B. 2014. "Etruscan Environments." In Turfa 2014:11–28.

INDEX